ISSUES MANAGEMENT IN STRATEGIC PLANNING

ISSUES MANAGEMENT IN STRATEGIC PLANNING

William L. Renfro

Quorum Books
Westport, Connecticut • London

Library of Congress Cataloging-in-Publication Data

Renfro, William L.
    Issues management in strategic planning / William L. Renfro.
      p. cm.
    Includes bibliographical references and index.
    ISBN 0-89930-785-X (alk. paper)
    1. Issues management. 2. Strategic planning. I. Title.
HD59.5.R46 1993
658.4′012—dc20   93-18244

British Library Cataloguing in Publication Data is available.

Library of Congress Catalog Card Number: 93-18244
ISBN: 0-89930-785-X

First published in 1993

Quorum Books, 88 Post Road West, Westport, CT 06881
An imprint of Greenwood Publishing Group, Inc.

Printed in the United States of America

∞™

The paper used in this book complies with the
Permanent Paper Standard issued by the National
Information Standards Organization (Z39.48—1984).

10 9 8 7 6 5 4 3 2 1

Contents

Figures

Acknowledgments

As with many lengthy personal projects, the final result includes the efforts of many people who supported and tolerated its creation. These include friends, colleagues and interns, especially Sandy Schlicker, Marc Griedinger, Howard Greene, Arthur Hull Hayes III, Gail Garey, Lisa Berman-Clough, Christine Keen, Eric Droutman, and Sophang Lim-You.

The contributions of these recent supporters were made possible by others who along the way provided the inspiration, leadership, and encouragement that produced the opportunity for this book. These have always been teachers of extraordinary abilities and substantial patience, especially O. Warren "Mac" McAdams, John B. Barclay, Dr. Robert W. Resnick, Dr. Clifford E. Davis, Wayne I. Boucher, Rev. George M. McAdams, John M. Reed, Rev. John C. Harper, the late Walter A. Hahn, Marvin Kornbluh, Dennis Little, and Hank Koehn. I thank them all.

ISSUES MANAGEMENT
IN STRATEGIC PLANNING

Introduction

Will the future happen *to* your organization, or *for* it? Will its leaders anticipate emerging issues with sufficient lead time to effectively and efficiently
manage its resources to create a strategic vision of better futures for itself, its
stakeholders, and its customers? The premise of this book is that concepts,
methods and procedures do exist which improve an organization's ability to
anticipate and manage emerging issues.

As both the legislative and executive branches have declined in their ability
to serve as a forum for the resolution of public issues, the role of the private
sector has grown. This shift of leadership from the public sector to the private is, for this quarter of the twentieth century, to equal the great changes
of each previous quarter-century: the birth of mass production in the first
quarter-century, the growth of centralized government in the second, and
the explosion of human and civil rights in the third.

As each private organization expands and improves its ability to anticipate
and respond to emerging public issues, it is helping to write a new constitution, a corporate constitution. This is a far more radical document than our
political constitution in its powers, speed, impacts, and lack of checks and
balances. How ironic that business, which feared and fought encroaching
powers of government, would be authoring so radical a document.

The issues-management process is fundamentally forward looking and
future oriented—a forecasting process. As more and more organizations
have found their fortunes determined as much, if not more, by external
issues than by internal forces, the importance and role of issues management
has grown.

Today, it is not stretching the truth at all to say that the private sector now plays a larger role in the public issues process than government. A new contract between business and the public is being written, one of a much greater social dimension. Issues management is the driving force of this fundamental shift in the roles of our largest institutions. The stakes could not be higher.

PART I

Issues Management: Origins, Concepts, and Models

1 ————————————————————

Issues Management: The Need

A sense of the future is behind all good politics. Unless we have it, we can give nothing either wise or decent to the world.

— C. P. Snow

THE RATIONALE OF LOOKING FORWARD

A sense of the future not only pervades all good politics but underlies every decision people make. People eat expecting to be satisfied and nourished — in the future. People sleep assuming that in the future they will be rested. They invest their energy, their money, and their time because they believe their efforts will be rewarded in the future. They build power systems assuming — or more correctly, forecasting — that a growing nation will need them in the future. People educate their children on the basis of forecasts that these children will want and need certain skills, values, ethics, and knowledge — in the future. In short, all humans make assumptions or implicit forecasts about the future to guide their daily decisions.

The question, then, is not whether people should, to the extent possible, seek to forecast the future, anticipating to the extent practical emerging issues, but whether they should articulate, discuss, analyze, and improve their forecasting and anticipating capabilities by using formal organizations and procedures and traditional management methods. The premise of explicit forecasting of emerging issues, threats, and opportunities is that by moving beyond their ordinarily unarticulated assumptions about the future, decision-makers can better guide their current decisions to produce a more desirable future state of affairs. It is a matter of whether executives will go into the future with their eyes and minds open or stumble into it with them closed. It is the contrast between rowing and sailing: rowing is good exercise, but a rower backs into his future, guessing his course by the view of where he has been. Using the wind, steam, or a team of rowers allows some small effort to be devoted to looking at the course ahead.[1]

The process of forecasting and anticipating emerging issues raises several fundamental problems. For example, understanding the nature of the universe, most humans realize that they can know nothing with absolute certainty about the future. But they can make some assumptions about the future that are so safe as to approach and be used like knowledge: when an election is expected to be held, when a project is scheduled to be completed, when a car will need replacement, when an electric power plant is forecast to need replacement, when a new technology is likely to come on line, when the life of everyone alive is likely to have ended, how purchasing patterns are likely to change if present social and economic trends continue, and so on. Knowledge in this weaker sense implies a possibility, sometimes high, sometimes low, that something may come along to upset the otherwise secure understanding (i.e., implicit forecast) of the future.

When people grant the presence of uncertainty, however slight, they are in the realm of forecasting. Forecasting is valuable and important, even when circumstances permit few — if any — degrees of real confidence in either the methods or the results they produce. Indeed, it is often far more important and valuable to focus on areas where confidence is low and where uncertainty — and the likelihood of upset — are high. Nowhere is this combination of low confidence and high uncertainty or upset more extreme than in forecasting emerging issues, especially those that may eventually stimulate public responses among customers, legislators, regulators, or any relevant part of the general public.

Future events that are almost certain to happen or almost certain not to happen are not very interesting unless, of course, they fail to turn out as expected. The "interesting future" includes such possibilities, but it also (more important) includes developments of middling probability whose occurrence or nonoccurrence will surely be decided within the period of interest as a result of decisions and policies implemented between now and then.

In a society and culture based on the scientific process of experimenting to develop and prove what is or can be known about nature, the process of thinking about the future and making forecasts stands alone in its vulnerability. Yet in spite of these risks and the unpredictability of the future, executives, like all other people, must constantly make assumptions about the future in guiding their ongoing decision processes, both personal and professional. Occasionally, of course, their assumptions are wrong, and they are surprised by sudden opportunities or developments that either create windfalls or provoke pain and loss. Nevertheless, as long as the future remains unpredictable, they have no choice but to go on making the best, most reliable assumptions and forecasts about the future that they can.

The future challenges the highly scientific society of twenty-first-century America in a unique way: the principles of science do not apply to the future. Scientists and researchers cannot run an experimental day from the year 2010. Thus, they cannot verify by experiment their theories about the future. While scientific research leads to laws that have predictive certainty, futures research leads to probabilistic forecasts and alternative scenarios. Professional futurists make the process of exploring possible futures as science-like in the rigor and discipline of its methods as possible, but they cannot turn the process into science. They cannot eliminate uncertainty. This is not to imply that they do not respect the scientific method: they do—they just cannot apply it.

As a society, Americans have accepted—usually grudgingly—the necessity of dealing with uncertainty in some aspects of their lives: a jury must find guilt "beyond a reasonable doubt"—not to a certainty; America's nuclear deterrence is based on the uncertainties of subatomic reactions ruled, in the end, by chance; travelers know (or have) some awareness of the odds— fatality rates—of the various forms of transportation and play the odds anyway; smoking "causes" cancer, but George Burns's cigars don't know that; seat belts save lives, but only nine times out of ten—there is a 10 percent chance of being killed in an accident because of a seat belt.[2]

In facing the uncertainty of the future, people use the best information available to reduce their fears, achieve a sense of control over the future, feel better about doing what they have to do—face uncertainty with incomplete information. The anticipating emerging issues and, more generally, the study of the future can reduce but not eliminate the perception of uncertainty.

Forecasting and the study of the future raise another major problem. Individual reputations, especially in business, are built and knowledge is based on following established rules and procedures of research and policy development that according to theory should lead to the same results regardless of the personalities involved.

If decision-making were a pure science, this would be true. However, as decision-making inevitably looks to and uses information about the future, it is not so simple. Information about the future cannot have this impersonality; it is all based on assumptions upon which reasonable persons can and do differ.

The information that forecasters generate about the future is fundamentally linked to their personal values, concepts, ideas, experience, outlook, and makeup. While issues management, forecasting, and futures research have to some extent borrowed detailed research methods and scientific concepts from other disciplines, these procedures cannot change the fundamental nature of postulating information about the future: it is an art, not a science. In the end, information about the future is based upon subjective human judgments. As a result, for executives whose lives, reputations, and careers rest on successful adherence to the traditional established rules and procedures, especially the clear and reliable ones of science and engineering, thinking about the future and making forecasts is uncomfortable, even threatening.

To think about the future and speculate about unknown and unknowable emerging issues is to challenge one of the keys to their success — careful use of "proper" research and decision-making methods. By recognized standards of every professional discipline, even the best information about the future is unacceptable, since it usually cannot meet traditional tests of objectivity, experimental verification, reproducibility, and so on. To traditional management teachings, the challenge is even more blunt: to the rule, "Don't decide in the dark, get all the facts first," the future says "You can only have all the facts when it's too late to decide anything." All information about the future may be judged inadequate in this light, but information about the future — almost *any* information about the future — is better than *no* information.

Anticipating emerging issues may be — and usually is — both inadequate *and* better than ignorance of them. It is a paradox of life that the only thing humans can know about is the past — but the only thing they can *change* is the future. Thus, they will always be lacking information — and seeking to improve what they do have — as they either base decisions on incomplete information or lose the opportunity to shape their futures.

This is not meant to imply that all information about the future is equal. It is not, and great care should be taken to always be conscious of the varying quality of information about the future. For example, since it takes fifty years to grow a fifty-year-old adult, the *maximum* possible population of fifty-year-olds is known for the next fifty years. With the highly stable and historically accurate actuarial data, demographers can forecast the *actual* expected population of this group for native-born Americans. Demographers have very high confidence in such forecasts. Their confidence falls sharply when they include legal and illegal aliens because the history here is neither notably stable nor necessarily indicative of the future.

U.S. courts have evolved a policy in admitting evidence that is useful to apply to forecasting future issues: the best-evidence rule. Simply put, an attorney is required to present the best available evidence to the court. For example, if the original of a document is available, a copy may not be submitted. If a person is available, an attorney may not submit a transcript, recording, or video of what the person said, no matter how well documented or certified, without presenting the person first.

The application of this policy to issues management requires only slight modification: not only do researchers use the best forecasts available, they use their best first, building from their strength into the softer and softer forecasts.

What is good information about future emerging issues? Simply put, it is information that helps decision-makers to improve their performance so they can achieve a better future than they believe would otherwise occur. Thus, total accuracy in the forecast cannot be the goal. By the time it is clear that the information about the future is correct—that is, has become a fact as noted above—it *must* be too late to do anything about it. Facts by definition have no uncertainty; similarly, the future is by definition uncertain.

For example, if air traffic controllers watching two planes on a radar screen develop a forecast with a new computer-projection technique that the planes will collide, the question to the responsible leaders is, "What should be done with this forecast?" They can wait, watching the radar screen to confirm the accuracy of their forecast when the planes in fact collide. But by the time they know their forecast was correct, they have permitted a catastrophe. This is not likely to be acceptable to the passengers on either of the planes, much less the general public. The forecast has value only if it is used by the appropriate leadership to intervene in the system to avoid the undesirable future of the catastrophe and direct the aircraft to safer courses—or more correctly, courses that are forecast to be safer.

This principle is just as valid for large complex issues and systems. For example, what should be done *now* to avoid the electrical shortages in the next century? What should be done *now* about the undernoted pension and Social Security funds for the retirement of the baby-boomers? What should be done *now* to avoid the problems of emerging issues likely to impact on corporations in the foreseeable future?

It is important to recognize that a forecast is usually a failure even if it turns out to be accurate. The Paley Commission appointed by President Truman in 1951 to study the long-term energy circumstances of the United States generated such a forecast.[3] The commission accurately forecast that the United States faced an energy crisis in the mid-70s. This forecast was a failure because it was not used to avoid that crisis. Thus, the key criterion must be that the forecast is used—*used* to create a better future than is otherwise anticipated.

To be used, the forecast must be communicated to the relevant decision-makers; and they must both believe what it suggests and have the resources, authority, and position to act on that information. Naturally, the accuracy of previous forecasts derived from similar methods or from similar forecasters or forecasting groups would enhance the credibility of subsequent forecasts from the same or similar sources—decision-makers will be more likely to assume that a method (or forecast) is credible if it has been accurate in the past.

This sort of externally derived credibility, however, is of limited value. Useful forecasts usually stand almost entirely on their own merits. In the case of the Paley forecast, the U.S. people and their political leaders simply were not convinced such a shortage could occur as they continued to enjoy abundant energy. The United States and virtually all other nations of the world face this same problem again as they returned to their wasteful, shortsighted ways. Clearly, the painful accuracy of the Paley forecast is not sufficient to stimulate more responsible actions even now.

Most forecasting is implicit, that is, unarticulated, and may appropriately remain so. Some forecasting should be articulated, discussed, debated, evaluated, challenged, changed, modified, and used in ongoing decision-making processes in an effort to achieve more desirable futures. The curse of Cassandra was to know the future but be powerless to change it. Forecasting gives executives their best information about the future, providing the opportunity for them to change it.[4]

THE INTERESTING FUTURE

Once the necessity to anticipate emerging issues of the future is recognized, a key question is, "Which future?" There are many futures — the likely future, the inevitable future, the necessary future, the official future, the desired future, the forgotten future, the manageable future, and so on. Collectively they makeup a rather large subject: The future is everything that will ever happen. That sounds so overwhelming it is difficult to know where to start. Yet the future is more than just what will happen, far more than this single path of what will ever happen, the future is everything that *could* ever happen — an infinity of possibilities.

The future is just too big — the decades, centuries, billions of years, each filled with millions of complex events — form an infinite array of possible futures. The vast majority of these possibilities are just not interesting to most executives now. These great infinities of the future must be brought down to a manageable size.

When a corporation addresses its future, it does not look out even a hundred years. The pace of change in its basic driving forces — politics, social change, new technologies — is so great that just a few decades into the future puts it into the realm of science fiction, far beyond the range of credible forecasting capabilities. At the same time, so much of what makes up the world today will change little in the next twenty, fifty, or even one hundred years. Thus, it is not possible or even useful to draw any arbitrary time line when looking to the future — the long-term future of one issue may be the short-term future of another. Since the important issues will not all fit into any single time span — the next five, seven, ten, fifteen years, or the decade five to fifteen years out — the life cycles of the issues themselves define the "interesting future." This concept is illustrated schematically in Figure 1.1

The time dimensions of the interesting future depend on the dynamics of the issue being addressed. In addressing the widespread use of a new technology only now in the prototype stage, then the interesting future may begin in a few years and extend a decade or decades into the future. In considering a legislative issue already at the hearing stage and facing mark-up, the interesting future may begin tomorrow and extend through the end of this session of Congress. A social trend may take decades to gain prominence. In each case it is the dynamics of the system within which the issue moves that deter-

Figure 1.1
The Interesting Future

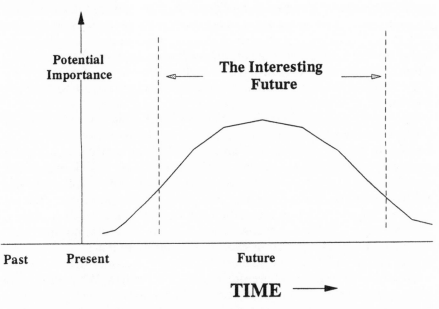

mines the time dimension. Usually, the interesting future extends two or three cycles of the issue's system into the future.

Time is only one of the dimensions of the interesting future. Items in executives' interesting future must have sufficient impact or potential for impact on their current or planned operations to command their attention and resources. Extremely probable and extremely improbable events are not usually very interesting, however great their potential impact. The modern world might come to a screeching halt if the genetic engineers let loose a bacterium that thrives on silicon chips—but this is so unlikely that executives may assume it will not happen. There are (it must be guessed) people in the Pentagon who do not make this assumption and who have just such a development in their interesting future.

This leads to another limiting dimension. Is an issue within the corporation's mission, purpose, or area of responsibility—whether its executives now can identify anything they might do about it or not? Will its customers, suppliers, regulators, or the public expect it to assume a leadership role on an issue—whatever this means when the issue emerges—even though today it has no reason to expect that it has the authority or resources for this purpose?

Much of the definition of this responsibility dimension, but not all, is derived from the expectation (forecast) that an issue is or can be responsive to the strategies and policies available to the corporate leadership today.

There is a delicate balance required here that is difficult to maintain. To make the investments necessary to support a new strategy or policy, a corporation needs a high degree of confidence in its forecast of the issue and of its ability to impact it. However, most issues become credibly foreseeable only when they have become so stable as to be impervious to outside forces, including those generated by a corporation's issue action program. In other words, by the time an executive has enough confidence in a forecast to justify expending his or her limited resources, it is often too late to have any real impact.

There are several other dimensions of the interesting future, more than can be shown in a three-dimensional perspective. For example, not all issues that fall into the time frame and have sufficient importance are part of the interesting future of any organization. Extremely improbable developments, as noted above, or the nonoccurrence of extremely improbable ones may not be interesting. Moreover, only those issues for which a corporation has either a responsibility or an expectation among some stakeholders to address qualify as part of the interesting future. Also, the corporation must have some authorization, implicit or explicit, to address an issue.

This authorization can be an elusive, subjective quantity that in the end rests in a highly judgmental decision by senior executives. While there is no body, group, or institution conferring authorization, it nevertheless is required. Such authorization comes from a nebulous public recognition that the corporation's legitimate interests are at stake in the resolution of the issue. (See Part VI for the role of standing in addressing issues.) Finally, the corporation must have the resources to mount an effective, efficient issue action program.[5]

These clear, if somewhat subjective, dimensions defining the interesting future notwithstanding, issues will appear in a corporation's future that defy all these measures and yet are very interesting. These singularities present the greatest challenge, for they are frequently defined only in retrospect with hindsight — they cannot be anticipated by any traditional means. Almost by definition, singularities are the exception to the rule: the past is prologue. In terms of the existing dimensions of the traditional interesting future, the singularities seem to appear from nowhere. To explain similar phenomena among elemental particles, physicists create imaginary "worm holes" in the space-time continuum through which these singularities travel unseen on the surface until they pop up in defiance of all other factors. Thus, a corporation finds itself, with little or no warning, suddenly confronting groups of angry, frightened employees divided over the issue of AIDS in the workplace. Or a customer suddenly turns a gun on customers and kills as many as he or she can. Or a killer tampers with a major national product, adding a highly toxic substance that kills several unsuspecting consumers. Singularities force the most rigorous, painful reassessment of the traditional judg-

Figure 1.2
The Interesting Future Revisited

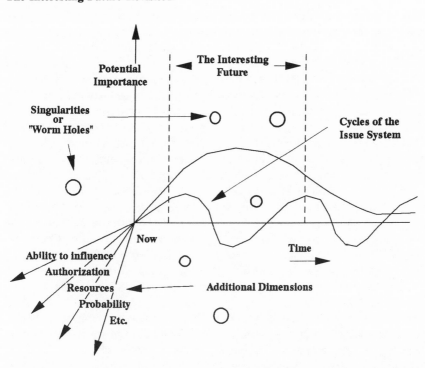

ments marking the dimensions of the interesting future. A complete sketch of the interesting future is shown in Figure 1.2.

In spite of these limiting dimensions, there remain many items in the corporation's interesting future — and new ones are constantly appearing. While the future may appear complex, chaotic, and confusing, it evolves in a reasonably orderly manner out of the trends, events, ideas, and actions of today. It is not knowable, but neither is it unknown. By careful scanning for the weak signals, senior management can identify key opportunities and threats in its interesting future in time to shape them to its advantage. This necessarily involves working with incomplete information — though it is the best available.

The bottom line is one of risk, more risk perhaps than executives are comfortable with, more risk than is tolerated in most traditional management functions. Yet the future presents executives with two options: either the leadership of a corporation takes by its own choice those risks essential to build the corporation's future, or it takes the risks of more and greater surprises from unforeseen emerging issues.

CHARACTERISTICS OF ISSUES

In the popular literature, issues take many different forms. They range from those with an extremely narrow, limited focus — of importance to only a few directly involved — to broad general topics such as the environment that reach virtually the entire public. A single, simple definition inclusive of all issues has not been developed in the professional literature and may not be necessary. Rather, a working definition of issues in terms important to issues-managers is essential. It requires a series of criteria.

Many subjects of national importance and concern cannot be described as issues. These areas of concern lack a key characteristic; no specific question or matter is in dispute. Nuclear war, the environment, and unemployment, among others, are areas of concern, not issues. There is no public group favoring or advocating nuclear war. None advocate the destruction of the environment nor unemployment. These areas of concern give rise to issues when alternative approaches to address them come into dispute — when the issues are joined. Each of the many concepts on how to best prevent nuclear war is an issue — thus the Strategic Defense Initiative is an issue, as is disarmament, SALT, START, and the nuclear freeze. Each proposal designed to limit or reduce environmental pollution is, or at least has the potential to be, an issue.

Thus, an issue must have at least two different possible resolutions. Moreover, there must be a dispute about which of the alternatives will prevail. A dispute necessarily requires at least two groups or parties who are sufficiently interested in or affected by the resolution of the issue to invest their resources in a struggle to prevail. Implicit in a dispute is a decision-point where one of the possible resolutions will be selected. These concepts are shown schematically in Figure 1.3.

For most issues, a decision-point must be of some relative proximity to the dispute. People and their organizations do not use their resources on disputes where there is no opportunity to effect change because a decision-point is not available.

For many issues, such as those linked with elections, there is a natural decision-point; but for many others have no such natural point. Of course, a group challenging the status quo or, to be more accurate, the current alternative being used or expected to be selected, may well focus its efforts on creating a decision-point by one of a variety of mechanisms. The democratic political process provides many opportunities to generate decision-points formally through legal action in the courts or through legislation in the Congress. Informal decision-points can be generated at other points in the public-issues process by issue advocacy tactics.

While decision-points can often be generated when they are not otherwise available, this is not always so. Some matters are closed, if by nothing more than the passage of time. The existence of most of the agencies created by

Figure 1.3
Characteristics of Issues

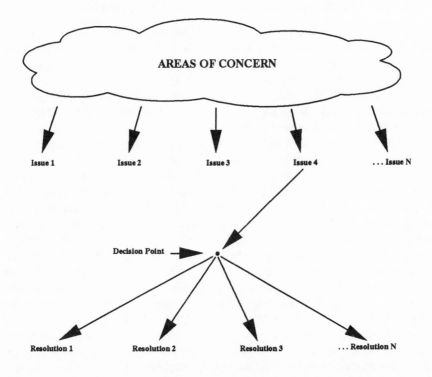

government were once hotly debated issues. While an agency may still occasionally stimulate a debate about its existence, as the Federal Trade Commission did repeatedly in the early 1980s, none has remained an issue.[6] Some issues are overtaken by events and die quite naturally and quietly. Many international issues born of the contest between east and west face this fate.

Perhaps most important in the United States is society's inability to resolve issues through any of the decision mechanisms. Some issues are constantly recycled to yet another decision-point. The abortion issues, for example, have been addressed by virtually every forum available—the legislature, the executive, the states, the courts, regulatory agencies—and it appears no closer to a resolution now than it ever was.[7]

Because of this inability to resolve them, society's list of issues is constantly growing. Since the dawn of the television age, only a few issues that did not have natural, irreversible decision-points, have reached anything close to a resolution. Except for Vietnam and Watergate, virtually every issue added to the national agenda in the past thirty years is still on the national issues agenda. There is no reason to believe the future holds any prospects for dramatic change.

THE STRUCTURE OF EMERGING ISSUES

In preparing his famous history of the eastern Mediterranean, Fernand Braudel discovered that he was writing three histories concurrently.[8] His first work followed day-to-day developments, recording the events and ongoing progress of the society. This history is the record of the events, the front page of an imaginary newspaper of this period, a history much like William Manchester's 1000-page book on the United States from 1932 to 1972, *The Glory and the Dream.*[9]

Braudel discovered that there is a second level of ongoing developments — the level of structural and institutional change. He realized that much of the surface history, or the indicators of surface change, depicted on the first level were driven by and dependent on this second level. Today, historians, economists, and politicians categorize unemployment as a key surface indicator; and they would give it much attention in writing a first history of current events. Over the past several decades, they have discovered that there are forces shaping unemployment — the structural and institutional changes occurring with the great increase in women entering or returning to the labor force and remaining in it and with modern western societies' evolution from a manufacturing, industrial economy to one based primarily on service and information sectors. If leaders want to understand the shifting demand and mix of employment in the country, they must understand the dynamics of baby-boom demographic forces, the changing family, and emerging personal roles. Interest rates, economic growth, government policies, and other surface factors alone cannot explain unemployment rates.

Finally, Braudel discovered that there is a third level of history, one derived from and focused on individual attitudes, values, and beliefs. He argues that these forces brought about changes on the institutional and structural level, which in turn brought about the changes in the surface indicators. These three levels — superficial, structural/institutional, and attitudinal — can be recursive (i.e., surface changes "cause" structural changes, which cause changes in values, which then cause changes on the other levels). Consider how commercially available, reliable, inexpensive birth control changed society's sexual values and how these value changes affected financial institutions: it was not so long ago that single women were denied mortgages and married women denied credit unless their husband cosigned.

The pace of change and the time period Braudel covered hid a fourth level of the future — one that can be seen today because of the faster pace of change, better communications, and longer, if not clearer, historical perspective. This level is philosophical in character. As the relationships between the other levels, a single change on this level can give rise to many changes

Figure 1.4
The Structure of the Future

	Surface Indicators	Structural/ Institutional Forces	Values/ Life Styles	Philosophies of Mankind
Social				
Technological				
Economic				
Legislative Regulatory Political				
Religion				

Note: The idea of explicitly adopting for futures research techniques developed by historians was first proposed by Wayne Boucher in conversation in 1975. The first three-level "Structure of the Future" was outlined by the author in 1979 and presented at the World Future Society Toronto conference in July 1980.

on the next level. Since the philosophical changes occur even more slowly than changes in values and lifestyles, changes—even over several decades— are subtle and difficult to delineate clearly. The four levels and their decreasing obviousness are shown in Figure 1.4.

Some part of American society, for example, has always been involved in conservation and acted responsibly toward the environment. Groups like the Boy and Girl Scouts, the Audubon Society, the Sierra Club, and other early conservation groups were committed for decades, but only since the first Earth Day, April 22, 1970, has this concern begun to reach more general publics. While subsequent events can be seen as a series of many changes in values, they can more succinctly be seen as the result of a change in philosophy from one perspective to another.

The original perspective was based on a philosophy and ethic rooted in the Old Testament direction God gave Adam and Eve — "the earth is yours and the fullness therein. Go forth and multiply." The earth was for the use and consumption of the human race. The emerging philosophy is based on a New Testament perspective — the earth does not belong to us to do with as we please. Rather it is a sacred trust for which each generation is responsible for preserving and protecting it so as to pass it on to the next generation in at least as good a condition, if not a better one. The management of a trust is based not on consumption and use but on the concept of stewardship. As distinguished from outright ownership of the first philosophy, this concept is one of a life estate — the life use of the inherited earth.

As with all life estates, there are limits on the use of its inheritance by any one generation — it must not be wasted, it must not be squandered. The first official recognition of the changing philosophy in the United States came in the 1990 White House Conference on Global Change: The subtitle and theme of the conference was "Global Stewardship."[10]

It is far too early to more than conjecture about other philosophical changes that may now be under way. As the philosophy governing mankind's relationship to the earth is changing, at least in the developed nations, so also the relationship between humans and their governments, as well as the human-to-human relationship and human-to-animal relationships, are also probably changing, though these changes have yet to be generally accepted by the public.

While it is impossible to place rigid time boundaries on the four levels of the future, here are the general fuzzy and overlapping boundaries of each level:

Time Frame (Years)	Level of the Future
1. 0–1	Surface Indicators
2. 1–7	Structural/Institutional Change
3. 5–20	Values/Life Styles
4. 10–100	Philosophies of Mankind

The vertical dimension of the Structure of the Future is a taxonomy of the issue space of concern to the corporation. Whatever terms are used, several simple objectives should be achieved: first, the list must be complete, with every foreseeable issue having a home; second, to the extent possible, each issue should have only one home or one primary home; and third, the terms should be descriptive of the contents of the category. At a very minimum, this taxonomy has four areas, denoted by the acronym STELR:

- Social
- Technological
- Economic
- Legislative/Regulatory

These four distinct areas, with several popular variations, were first identified and widely used in the technology assessment movement. Some taxonomies included "environmental issues" in a separate category, even though these issues could almost always be classified by their major area of impact in other categories. Some variations used the term "politics" to describe legislative/regulatory change, though history shows little correlation between the two—for example, Republican presidents signed most of the social protection legislation of the last thirty years.

Any number of different generic categories have been proposed and used. EPISTLE is one that has enjoyed some following: Economic, Political, Institutional, Social, Technical, Legislative, Environmental. The goal of a taxonomy is that every emerging issue has a place, but only one place, in the taxonomy. Depending on the nature of the emerging issues being considered, many different taxonomies might be used.

For the purposes of establishing the concept of the Structure of the Future, four categories are adequate. Of course, every corporation will want to develop its own much more detailed taxonomy, with categories reflecting and defining its unique issues space. These categories are usually developed during issues assessment/environmental audit stage of a scanning process (see Chapter 5).

The Structure of the Future implies, however subtly, that the changes occurring among the STELR components are equal. They are not. Frequently, technology changes arrive most rapidly. In the past, a popular adage held that what was in the labs today would be on the market in 10 years. Today, that time horizon has shrunk to something much shorter. U.S. car manufacturers now target (and Japanese makers now produce) a completely new motor vehicle—*car* is too limited a term for the world of mini-vans, APVs, compact pick-ups, and the like—in 3.5 years. Electronic products are lucky to have a market life of 3.5 years as product innovation runs in months. Children's toys have markets lives of months or even weeks. Technology issues follow on a similar high-speed track.

Economic issues often place a close second to technology. In spite of the growing size of the world economy, the pace of change, especially of financial issues, has reached the limits of human ability to manage. Here, the invisible hand of technological is at work as computers and satellite communications merge into *compu*nications, melding regional and national markets into a single whole. Governments lose control over their own currencies, monetary policy, financial resources, economic growth, and issues.

Figure 1.5
The Law of Social and Technological Change

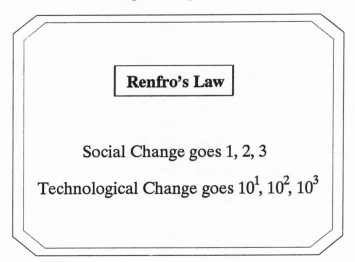

Renfro's Law

Social Change goes 1, 2, 3

Technological Change goes $10^1, 10^2, 10^3$

"Time once was when we could prepare a person for a life-long career. Today, however, the pace of change has reached such an astounding pace that we must continually re-educate ourselves for an ever changing environment."[11] It has been more than sixty years since Sir Alfred North Whitehead's observation on the "astounding pace of change." While society does not change as rapidly as either technology or the economy, its pace of change remains astounding even today. This pace of change led Alvin Toffler to the conclusion that our entire society is experiencing the equivalent of the shock experienced by moving geographically from one culture to another—only for us time provides the movement as we experience "Future Shock."[12]

While many executives experience the legislative/regulatory world as an area of rapid change, our legislative institutions are in fact laggards. Only after society's need for legislative or regulatory change is clear, after every possible interested party has testified at one or more of the many hearings, and a majority of the interested public has become irreversibly committed to change will legislators risk even the most timid change. Only those who ignore the ongoing, highly public legislative and regulatory process experience its slow, timid movement as a source of rapid, unforeseen change. It simply cannot be that when business wants something from legislatures, "it takes forever," while some other groups are able to move their wants at the pace of surprises.

The differential pace of change of social and technological issues gives rise to battles that are often fought in either the legislative or economic spheres—or both. Since the differences in pace between social and technical change

Figure 1.6
The Structure of the Interesting Future

Surface Indicators	Structural/ Institutional Forces	Values/ Life Styles	Philosophies of Mankind

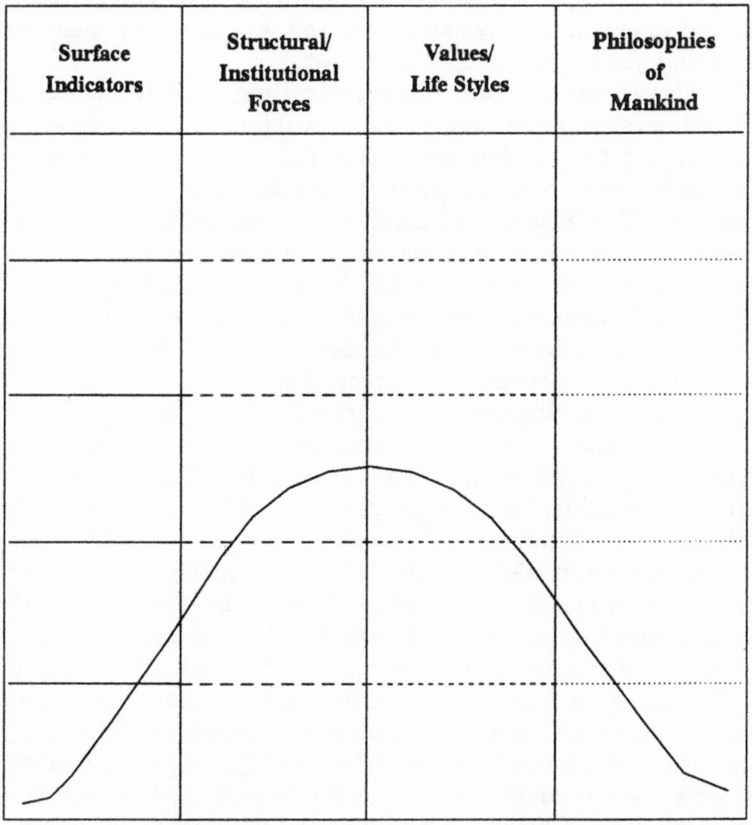

are the source of so many issues, these differences are worth noting in "Renfro's Law" (Figure 1.5).

In the context of issues management, the interesting future is most likely to be centered on the first two levels. However, the second two levels must be included in any comprehensive issues management program to develop and maintain the necessary strategic perspective on emerging issues. The relationship between the two concepts can be seen in Figure 1.6.

EVOLUTION OF THE EMERGING ISSUES CONCEPT

Braudel's levels of history, as expanded, may also serve as a means for viewing the future. Early forecasting and futures research methods focused on indicators and measures of surface change, such as unemployment, inflation, economic growth, sales of automobiles, housing starts, and the like.

Most discussions of the future still focus on these surface indicators, usually using implicit forecasts. For example, on the center front page of the *Wall Street Journal* every day is a historical chart of some surface indicator from which readers may implicitly make their own forecasts. This chart thus establishes an unarticulated, implicit forecast.

Given this view of the future, it is not surprising that futures research and forecasting developed and used a host of extrapolative methods in support of long-range planning that were focused on surface indicators. These methods included regression analysis, mathematical and judgmental trend extrapolation, Box-Jenkins, rolling averages, and so forth. The focus of this traditional long-range planning was an internal one, based on tracking and forecasting developments internal to an organization or system.

As surprise developments continued to upset the forecasts and long-range plans produced by these methods, forecasters modified them to take explicit account of unprecedented new developments and external "surprises." While many of these were surprises on the surface, futures researchers began increasingly to include changing developments on the structural and institutional level. Thus, trend extrapolation was modified to become trend impact analysis, a probabilistic forecasting technique in which an extrapolative trend is modified by the occurrence of hypothesized external surprise events.

At the same time, models of large national and global economies created via systems dynamics—the method popularized by The Club of Rome's *Limits to Growth*—were modified to include similar external surprises.[13] While the first generation models assumed fixed relationships among variables, the next generation allowed relationships to change in response to external developments, events, and surprises. With this modification, *probabilistic* systems dynamics was born.[14] Relationships among external surprise events were also explored through such methods as cross-impact analysis.

In the mid-1970s, a method for guiding the development of responses to information about the future on the first two levels was developed—policy impact analysis (PIA).[15] Traditional forecasting produces explicit information about futures but leaves the decision-maker with only implicit guidance on what to do with the new information. Policy impact analysis takes the results of probabilistic forecasting as a launch pad to develop specific policy responses to create better futures. Simply put, a policy in the PIA process is an event that it made happen. The decision-maker, of course, is the source of candidate policies, as well as the ultimate authority on how and when they impact on the future. When the policies are added to the model, the outlook for the future changes—for the better if the policies are successful. Further evaluation leads not only to the most effective policies but also to the most cost-efficient ones. Now the decision-maker not only has more information about the future, but better yet, he or she knows what to do with it.

Today, methods are in use that will take account of information from the third level of the future—changing values and attitudes. But these methods are in their infancy in this application, and their users frequently have no clear idea of what balance should be struck among potential developments on all three levels. Coping seriously with this question is one of the frontiers of issues management in particular and futures research in general. Incidentally, while it is, of course, possible today to approach this question through opinion research, opinion research has been notoriously weak in forecasting, for the simple reason that individuals' judgments about their future attitudes and opinions have proven very unreliable—unreliable in comparison to their reports about their current attitudes.

The real difficulty with polling and opinion surveys designed to forecast the future, however, is not that individuals are unreliable; it is that pollsters who have tried forecasting (something rarely done, by the way) have sought predictive accuracy. They have not sought to obtain information useful for managing change and increasing their options, but rather to describe a predestined, fixed future. Thus, they have targeted issues that would prove the accuracy of their methods rather than the value of those methods. Trying to predict future surface indicators such as inflation, unemployment, and interest rates on the basis of opinion is no more useful than "trying to predict which way a kitten will jump next," as H. G. Wells put it in 1903.[16]

As futures research and forecasting methods were becoming less and less quantitative and more qualitative, the process of exploring and responding to changing social structure and values (the second and third levels of the future) was becoming more and more important. For example, the traditional "fire fighting" mode of public relations was modified to include a planning or forecasting role in what became known as public affairs. This role was extended to include policy planning. Thus, it is not unusual to find on a contemporary corporate organizational chart a director of public policy planning, a position stationed philosophically somewhere between the traditional public relations–government relations–public affairs function and the corporate planning function. In some organizations the policy planning function has been extended to include a director of public issues, who has the responsibility of anticipating and helping the organization to respond to emerging public issues in the external environment.[17]

The field of issues management emerged as public relations or public affairs officers included more and more forecasting and futures research in their planning and analysis of policy. The new field of issues management is emerging both from the evolution of futures research methods from quantitative to more qualitative aspects and from the development in the public relations field that is shifting from qualitative to more quantitative methods. The merger of futures research concepts and techniques into the public policy planning function holds the prospect that administrators will eventually pay close attention to detailed information about the future on all these levels.

Currently the most common technique used for including more information about the external world from both the second and third levels (i.e., structural and institutional change and changing values and lifestyles) is environmental scanning. As with earlier forecasting techniques, scanning focused first on the surface indicators—newspapers, literature, periodicals—as signals of underlying change in the more difficult to understand institutional, structural, values and lifestyles levels. Refinements in and new methods of environmental scanning must be developed. While a small scan of the external environment usually was made to identify candidate surprise events, the focus remained on the trends and issues developed from the traditional, internal perspective. The addition of the external perspective redefines the long-range planning process with its internal perspective to a strategic planning process with both internal and external perspectives.

For a few select issues, the emerging issues process matures on through advanced stages, finally culminating in new federal legislation. Depending on the stage at which an organization becomes involved or is involved in an issue, the "issue" may have as its focal point of definition everything from a first defining event to the final legislation. The pension reform issue, for example, began with the bankruptcy of Studebaker and its pension fund and ended with President Ford signing the Employee Retirement Income Security Act (ERISA) fourteen years later. For most corporations, the "issue" was not retirement income security but compliance with the funding standards imposed by ERISA itself. A relative of this issue survives today as Congress considers similar standards for public employee retirement programs.

In the 1980s, Congress continued to wrestle with issues of day care—financing, standards, liability, quality, and other factors. The underlying trends are continuing—mothers increasingly working outside the home, the need for two incomes, and the like. It would be naive to expect that all this work will come to nothing. The only credible forecast must be that eventually Congress will establish federal requirements and standards for day care providers, at least for corporations with fifty or more employees.

As the legislative response means so much, it is important to understand the process of moving issues forward from changing values to final legislation and regulations. This process is addressed in Chapter 2.

2

Modeling the Public Issues Process

When the Industrial Revolution began, the dominant paradigm of management in industry was the single genius-entrepreneur. Such individuals forged great enterprises through their personal brilliance and accomplishments. Soon the complexities of the industrialized society became too great for any single person, however talented, to manage. A new style of management emerged: the committee, the system, quite literally, the Sloan School. When General Motors under Alfred Sloan overtook the Ford Motor Company under the single genius Henry Ford, this transition reached its pinnacle.

In these major organizations, a new form of management is challenging the old, and the new paradigm is a participatory style of management. This is not a benign internal participation of employees throughout the organization under the guidance of an enlightened senior management but a confrontational demand by those outside the organization who inject their participation into its most private, traditionally internal decisions. This participation is accomplished through the medium of public issues and the responses they generate through public opinion, attitudes, government, and legal and other forums.

This participatory management paradigm began to emerge in the 1970s. In the first two hundred years of the U.S. government, some thirty-five major social protection laws were enacted by the Congress, of which only seven antedated 1960.[1]

While Americans were publicly debating and, for the most part, rejecting the womb-to-tomb socialism of "government is responsible for all aspects of their lives," they quietly have applied a version of this to the private sector —

Major U.S. Social "Protection" Legislation

1877	Dangerous Cargo Act
1893	Safety Appliance Acts
1906	Federal Food, Drug, and Cosmetic Act
1906	Federal Meat Inspection Act
1954	Atomic Energy Act
1957	Poultry Products Inspection Act
1958	Federal Aviation Act
1960	Federal Hazardous Substances Act
1966	National Traffic and Motor Vehicle Safety Act
1968	Radiation Control for Health and Safety Act
1969	Federal Mine Safety and Health Act
1969	National Environmental Policy Act
1970	Poison Prevention Package Act
1970	Occupational Safety and Health Act
1970	Clean Air Act
1970	Federal Railroad Safety Act
1971	Lead Based Paint Poisoning Prevention Act
1971	National Cancer Act
1972	Federal Insecticide, Fungicide, and Rodenticide Act
1972	Consumer Product Safety Act
1972	Marine Protection, Research and Conservation Act
1972	Ports and Waterways Safety and Health Act
1972	Federal Water Pollution Control Act
1972	Marine Protection Research and Sanctuaries Act
1972	Noise Control Act
1973	Endangered Species Act
1974	Safe Drinking Water Act
1975	Rail Safety Improvement Act
1975	Hazardous Materials Transportation Act
1976	Toxic Substances Control Act
1976	Solid Waste Disposal Act
1976	Resource Conservation and Recovery Act
1977	Surface Mining Control and Reclamation Act
1979	Hazardous Liquid Pipeline Safety Act
1980	Comprehensive Environmental Response, Compensation and Liability Act (Super Fund)

corporations, not-for-profits, and other institutions—even to the services, operations, and actions of federal, state, and local government agencies. Now, in response to issues brought by management's new participants, public opinion—speaking through the public issues process—regulates every stage of the developing, designing, constructing, manufacturing, selling, labeling, disposing of, hiring, firing, compensating, pensioning, and virtually all other aspects associated with providing a product or service, whether in the private, nonprofit, or public sector. To the extent that government agencies provide services similar to those provided by private sector institutions, they are subject to the same forces of change; and in the context here, they are included in this discussion. Where a corporation, institution, or agency fails to respond to the public issues process "voluntarily," federal or state regulations can and, in most cases, will eventually force a response acceptable to the general public.

People in the industrialized nations of the West do not think of corporations, not-for-profit organizations, and government agencies as democratic institutions that must follow and anticipate the will of the people as it is expressed through issues of concern to them. However, this anticipation, through issues, is forcing these institutions to become as responsive as—and in many ways, far more responsive than—their traditional democratic institutions designed to deal with social change—their federal, state, and local governing bodies. The private sector has always been (and to many still is) private; by definition, the public sector is "the people's business."

A new contract for the private sector is being written, this one (between the people and business) is primarily a social rather than economic contract. It makes their old social contract with government—the Constitution with its Bill of Rights, amendments, and latter day Supreme Court interpretations—seem very conservative. How ironic it is that business, forever concerned about the encroachment of socialism perspectives via the political process, is now itself living under a constitution wherein such perspectives are not even issues—they are basic assumptions.

Just as successful politicians must respond to their constituents, so successful executives must anticipate and respond to the issues and opinions of importance not just to their constituents—their customers, their suppliers, their employees—but to any public that would like to participate in their decision-making. Unlike the elected politician who works within a certain known structure—elections on a schedule with relatively clear, stable duties of office—and with certain basic rights—innocent until proven guilty, notice of new laws and requirements, and so forth—today's executive faces a fluid structure, the retroactive application of new standards without even minimum notice, and few, if any, basic rights. The principles and rules of the private constitution have never even been committed to paper, no doubt because they would be terrifying.

The new constitution's requirements are not limited to the private sector. Whole nations must live by the same rules. Uncertainty about the future of a country will quickly kill all new foreign investment—with far faster and greater impact than could ever be achieved through traditional foreign policy institutions. Neither the Contras nor the official U.S. trade boycott, embargoes, and restrictions hurt the Sandinistas nearly so much as private sector forces when tourism and investment vanished. When Jamaica elected an avowed Marxist, tourism—with its influx of hard currency—evaporated even before an inauguration was held. Similarly, once Atlanta earned the dubious title of murder capital of the United States, it suddenly found its convention business devastated, with its newest and largest complex, The Omni, filing for bankruptcy protection. The fire in the Happyland after hours social club in New York City sent mayors across the land scurrying to close their illegal after hours clubs.[2]

By 1982 the new private contract's democratic demands on private sector management became so great that Robert O. Anderson, then chairman of the Atlantic Richfield Oil Company (ARCO) observed:

Failure to perform competently and credibly in the realm of public issues can be devastating to the prospects of any business. In fact, it is not stretching fact at all to say that business today has a new bottom line—public acceptance. Without the approval and support of society, it is obvious that financial success is irrelevant.[3]

Initially, corporations, not-for-profit organizations, associations, and even government agencies themselves responded to the new paradigm by incorporating more and more information about their external environments into their traditionally internally oriented long-range planning. It may seem odd that government executives would be interested in this subject, but of course government must live by its own new rules—if not lead the way by setting an example—just like everybody else. Thus a new environmental law that clobbers a corporation or an entire industry may be just as devastating to the budgets and operations of government agencies that are its customers. In 1992, the Environmental Protection Agency, for example, had difficulty meeting its own standards for indoor air quality in the offices of its national headquarters. Certainly the twenty-eight laws enacted since 1960 have cost the government itself billions of dollars. In addition to dealing with these impacts, issues managers in government agencies have a special problem in the United States—they are prohibited by law from direct advocacy or traditional lobbying of the Congress. While this limitation restricts their participation on many wide-ranging issues, they have special access to Congress on issues within their jurisdiction through the appropriation and authorization processes.[4]

Recognizing the changing paradigm and the necessity for better information about the future, the Congress decided to undertake these functions

Figure 2.1
The Strategic Planning Process

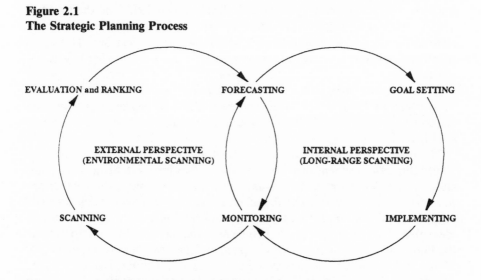

EVALUATION and RANKING   FORECASTING   GOAL SETTING

EXTERNAL PERSPECTIVE
(ENVIRONMENTAL SCANNING)

INTERNAL PERSPECTIVE
(LONG-RANGE SCANNING)

SCANNING   MONITORING   IMPLEMENTING

itself. In 1974 it established in its procedural rules a "foresight provision" requiring its committees to study the future.[5]

Eventually the pace and prominence of external change became so great that adding external issues to internal perspectives of the future was no longer satisfactory: a new external perspective was also required. Leaders of organizations simply found that outside participants were having as much impact on the future of their organizations as they were, or more. By the late 1970s, CEOs reported they were spending an average of 50 percent of their time on external issues. By one estimate, this had grown to 70 percent by the mid-1980s.[6] A balance between internal and external perspectives became a measure of the new paradigm. In a sense this marked the birth of the field called issues management.

To respond to this new paradigm, management at first formed special, high-level issues management working groups. Corresponding groups in government were known as foresight teams. Although they were originally formed to manage responses to particular issues, the continuous emergence of new issues soon made this a permanent function. Today, more than half of America's largest corporations have issues management functions operating under a variety of names and organizational styles. Congress formed The National Foresight Network,[7] and Congressional Research Service formed a foresight team.[8] In 1982 two dozen founding practitioners of this new function met with eighty of their colleagues at the Library of Congress to form the Issues Management Association (IMA). In the late 1980s, branches of IMA were formed in Canada and the United Kingdom.

Shifting the management paradigm to a participatory one is based on several principles that guide the development of issues (see Figure 2.1). With both the interconnectedness of modern developed societies and the flood of instant communications, issues develop wide-ranging impacts and move transnationally — at the speed of each country's communications. This high-speed movement is scarcely limited by political borders or the boundaries of the initiating problem: the greatest pressure on South Africa comes not from within but from without; the first major anti-Shah demonstration took place in Washington, not Teheran; the anti-Nestlé-infant-formula boycott occurred in the United States, even though the product was never sold here.

The many issues with both wide impact and high-speed development or transnational movement provide the lessons that have established the principles of issues management. So many issues have moved from the first appearance of public concern to the enactment of government legislation and regulation that the major stages of the issues management process can be identified. This allows the process to be anticipated. It is this anticipation of the likely future requirements of government legislation and regulations that is shifting the democratic process of resolving major public issues from the political arena to the corporate boardroom and other private management forums. Unencumbered by the complex procedures of the political process — with all its protections, checks, and balances — but operating under the new set of rules, private decision-makers can, must, and do anticipate and respond much faster than their political counterparts. The constitution of the new social contract — and the survival of these organizations — requires it.

This de facto shift in power from the political arena to the private sector — changing the economic contract to a social one and creating a de facto private sector constitution — is the most important political and management development of the last quarter of this century. In its long-term societal impacts, it will eventually rival the great developments of the first three quarters of this century: the father of manufacturing — the assembly line, the New Deal, and the civil rights movement. How much more ironic it is that business is now itself the major mechanism implementing the dreaded concepts of such a radical social document — albeit from prospects of enlightened self-interest.

THE ISSUES LIFE CYCLE

A key to the entire concept of issues management is the premise that the development of public issues can be anticipated by comparison with the behavior of similar issues in the past. This concept is based on the recognition that issues moving and developing within a given framework, whether major national or international issues, state or local issues, specific industry or product issues, pass through particular stages regardless of their subject or content. The life cycle of the issues in a system is a characteristic of the system itself rather than the issue. This is analogous to the product life cycle in which products of a given generic kind or family are all observed to pass through the same stages.[9]

The stages and timing of issue systems vary significantly, though they all appear to be running faster and faster. The concept that public issues have a life cycle, developed in the late 1970s, has grown in acceptance, utility, and complexity over the past decade. Today, several major models describe the different paths of development that national public issues may follow. They all are based on concepts originating in the late 1970s in private research reports and subsequently detailed in several professional journals and international conferences.[10]

As with the structure of the future, developments on the surface can be traced to changing societal values. While the birth of an issue has rarely ever been witnessed, it happens very frequently in the fertile ground of changing societal values. When it happens, it is often obscure and mired in the confusion of controversy. It is often unclear in the chicken-and-egg world of controversy and changing values, which comes first. Controversy, though, almost always seems to be present as issues are born. The reason is no more profound than that not all people change values at the same time. Different values lead to different visions of the future with different goals. The struggle over different goals generates controversy. In a democratic republic with a free market for ideas, the marketing of ideas defines the struggle for the future. The very nature of the process encourages advocates of new visions and goals to generate as much attention as possible as a means of promoting their position. The art of manipulating the media via controversy, real or apparent, has evolved to a profession: Lois Gibbs, one of the mothers who organized the Love Canal community, left her family after the Love Canal issue faded to open a Washington consulting company using the tactics she used there.[11]

It is simply too universal to claim that all emerging issues have their origins in changing, redefined, or restated societal values. Certainly, some issues arise without any apparent change in values but provide an opportunity for the expression of well-established existing values. Three Mile Island defined public concern over nuclear safety that was well established a decade earlier. The nuclear safety issue, however, has its roots in changing values and attitudes toward the environment, distrust of technology, and suspicion of government. The resignation of President Nixon and the Watergate affair may well not have involved any significant change in ethical values—if the people had known of similar conduct of another president in the past, a similar result might well have been obtained. This may touch on the very change in values that brought Nixon down—what the people expected to know about the actions of their president and government.

If nothing more, the experience of Vietnam made the media and the people highly suspicious of official information provided by the White House in particular and by the government and all in authority in general. Had the people's values not shifted from one of trust to one of suspicion, it is doubtful that Watergate would have ever happened. This has nothing to do with the break-in but with the consequences of Nixon's efforts to cover up the entire affair. Without the uncovering by the *Washington Post's* reporters Woodward and Bernstein, the administration might have succeeded in the cover-up. However, the uncovering is not sufficient: the public had to suspect government in general, and Nixon in particular, of deception and find this deception unacceptable by the ethical standards of the emerging post-Vietnam era.

Presidential deception was not new in 1974. The media had at times even been a willing participant in deception, covering up or not uncovering official and personal misconduct. To a real extent, the media reflected the values of the public that simply did not want to know too much about the clay feet of its leaders. After Lyndon Johnson's deceptions over Vietnam were uncovered by the escalating human and economic costs, public values changed. The people increasingly suspected the worst and wanted to know every detail. The media, feeling they had been duped by Kennedy's charm and Johnson's deceptions into a role of unwitting coconspirator, struggled to regain their reputation and independence. Johnson felt the heat first and withdrew; but "Tricky Dick" Nixon charged ahead, seemingly made for his part in confirming America's worst suspicions about its government while restoring the media to their historic role as watchdogs for the people, critics of the government.

While the order may vary after the birth of an issue, the early stages of the issues development process include these:

Birth: in changing personal or social values, new technologies, new impacts, social change, and the like

Definition: an event that defines and focuses the issue in the public's mind

Name: the development and acceptance of a single word or phrase to identify all aspects of an issue — for example, Watergate

Champion: a person or persons who campaign the issue much like a politician with press conferences, books, and planned media events

Group: formal or informal groups of various publics who decide to participate in the issue process

Media Recognition: first local, then regional and national, the key step that moves an issue up the public agenda, enhancing its priority over competing issues

Issue Definition. While the changing societal values that give birth to issues are obscure, murky, and often unrecognized at the time, the next step is anything but unclear: a defining event. For many issues, changing societal values go unrecognized until some sudden, unforeseen event or sharp discontinuity galvanizes the public. Often, issues (like public exposure to hazardous wastes) remain unfocused, smoldering on the national-issues "back burner" until a single event, a single place, some specific injuries, real victims are defined by a clear, unequivocal development such as Love Canal. For the nuclear power industry, it was Three Mile Island. For air safety, it was the DC-10. The ever present crime issue is frequently redefined by the latest crime of exceptional shock value – the New York jogger, the Manson murders, Bensonhurst, Ted Bundy, the Scarsdale Diet Doctor, the Son of Sam, or some other *cause celebre*.

For auto safety, it was the Corvair and later the Pinto. Most recently, Audi has seen the destructive power of issues mismanagement as its weekly U.S. sales went from an average of almost 240 cars to fewer than 30 after Audi stumbled over the sudden-acceleration issue. Audi's fate was not unlike that of Corvair. Ralph Nader's attack on the Corvair led to the formation of the National Highway Traffic Safety Administration. The uniform reporting of accident data by NHTSA later exonerated the Corvair: NHTSA found no evidence the Corvair suffered any unique safety defect – Nader's claims were unsubstantiated. NHTSA was unable to find any flaw in the Audi, either.

Like the Corvair, the Audi was denounced by Nader through a New York public interest group for being unsafe. Though some 700 incidents of sudden acceleration had been reported to NHTSA, only a couple involved Audis. Nevertheless, after the media took up Nader's call, including a *60 Minutes* segment featuring a faked demonstration similar to NBC's famous GM truck fire, Audi was marked to take the fall on the sudden-acceleration issue.

Perhaps due to the Quixotic manner in which Audi became the target, it failed to respond to the issue other than to release a technical report concluding "there is nothing wrong with the car: the driver stepped on the gas, not the brake." Audi owners and potential Audi owners found this far less than acceptable. If Audi had issued a prompt recall of the affected models for safety tests instead of maintaining its stony silence, it would have cost Audi far less than the loss of more than 80 percent of its U.S. market. Eventually Audi ran full page ads in all the major national newspapers under the heading, "It's Time We Talked"; but by then, it was well past that time. Audi, a first rate car with legendary engineering and innovation, was badly damaged in its market sector. Not even a guaranteed repurchase plan was able to revive sales as much as five years after the debacle. Current Audi owners are stuck with cars having about half the fair resale value. Again, there is no evidence that the Audi ever suffered from any unique safety defect. Moreover, several other makes of cars have been accused of having sudden acceleration accidents much more frequently. Manufacturers of competing models quietly equipped their cars with interlocks, requiring the driver to step on the brake to get the transmission out of PARK.

Issue Name. The name given an issue need not be rational or even particularly descriptive. The fall of President Nixon was named after a Washington hotel – Watergate. This name was so powerful that subsequent political scandals have all had as candidate names some kind of "gate." The scandal over Reagan's access to Carter's briefing papers became "brief-gate." The Iran-arms-sales, Contra-funding scandal became "Iran-gate." Clearly, those with a vested interest in creating a Watergate-like scandal saw some advantage in invoking the image and memory of Watergate, whether it fit or not. In the end, since the issues either died or took on other names, the public did not find another Watergate in the events.

The name of an issue is or can be of great importance. Most issue advocates try to be *for* something the society values and use a name to steer, shape, or focus the issue to their advantage. Thus, both sides of the abortion issue are pro-something—pro-life versus pro-choice. Recognizing the power a name can carry, the media occasionally weigh in with a heavy-handed attempt to name an issue. On the abortion issue, for example, the *Washington Post* requires its reporters to call the pro-life and right-to-life groups "anti-abortionists" and pro-choice groups "reproductive rights advocates," according to its official "style manual."[12]

To the extent a name does define a given issue, it is important—and often controversial. The names of the abortion issue determine whether it is an issue of human life or human rights. People who have no housing are called "homeless" by their supporters, though having housing—physical shelter from the elements—and having a home—a family residence—are two quite different matters. Millions of people who have quite adequate, even luxurious housing, have no homes.

The fast food industry struggles to avoid the junk food label. The alcohol industry struggles to keep alcoholism out of the drug and substance abuse issue. President Reagan tried to name his Strategic Defense Initiative the "Peace Shield," but "Star Wars" was much more popular. Margaret Thatcher's downfall was attributed in large part to the public support she lost over local tax reform, which became known as a "poll tax," evoking dreaded images of past inequities—even though her reform was in no way a poll tax in the sense that term is commonly understood.[13] The power of defining an issue is discussed later.

Often, a sudden or unexpected event will define an issue with little or no debate. Until Chernobyl came along, Three Mile Island defined the nuclear safety issue. Prior to TMI, "Seabrook" was the leading candidate name for this issue. Khe San became the name for America's frustration in Vietnam, as My-Lai expressed the horror of it all.

Issue Champions. Frequently, an issue emerges from the work of a single issue champion or advocate who writes a book. Dr. Rachel Carson brought the impact of humans on the environment to public attention with her 1962 book *The Silent Spring*. Betty Freidan heralded the emergence of feminist issues and the feminist movement with her 1970 book, *The Feminine Mystique*. Ralph Nader's *Unsafe at Any Speed* gave birth to the auto safety issue. Many other advocates have written books to define and promote their issues.

This is, of course, not a new idea but a great tradition in American history. At the turn of the century, Upton Sinclair's book, *The Jungle,* defined the food safety issue. In 1847, Richard Henry Dana wrote in the preface to *Two Years before the Mast* that the purpose of his book was to increase "public awareness of the plight of seamen." And it simply violates *Common Sense* to ignore the contribution Thomas Paine made in 1775.

Books are not the only way to champion an issue. Peter and Susan Hibbard, New Jersey science teachers, found a dead sea turtle on the beach a few years ago. They decided to do an autopsy. In its stomach, they found the remains of a balloon which, they decided, was part of a runaway helium balloon that caused the death of the turtle. In 1985, scientists at the Marine Mammal Stranding Center found balloon remains in a dead whale. While they have not yet written a book, they did form the Balloon Alert Project for teachers and students to protest balloon releases. Their efforts in the press did lead directly to legislation banning the release of helium balloons in four states and a 30 percent drop in a $1-billion-a-year industry.[14]

Issue Groups. No sooner is an issue defined than a group is formed to advocate a particular resolution. Americans love to join causes, whether defined by formal groups or informal. Whether amorphous social phenomena such as the antiwar, civil rights, and environmental movements or highly organized memberships such as the National Organization for Women, NAACP, Greenpeace, and the like, every issue has one or more groups behind it. Public issue groups (PIGs) or single issue groups (SIGs) have grown from a cottage industry to the largest employer in Washington save government.

Some groups stumble into being from grassroots incidents, while others are carefully created with ample resources to define and market an issue. Almost every idea, forum, and mechanism has been tried by those seeking to form an issue group. An unhappy car buyer found himself head of a group after he expressed his anger in a newspaper advertisement. Usually, of course, staging a "defining event" to promote an issue via media attention is a carefully planned, intentional act. Computer networks and bulletin boards are becoming increasingly popular mechanisms for surfacing and debating issues.

Often, individuals are unaware that others are in the same or similar circumstances and that they share common needs and goals with many others. Unforeseen developments often create groups such as those formed by the women injured by the Dalcon Shield IUD or the relatives of those killed by the bombing of Pan Am Flight 103.

More often than not, the issue group begins with volunteer membership. Recently, the effect of groups has been increased by two new tactics. High school students in Aurora, Colorado, not even close to the nearest Pacific dolphin, started the boycott of tuna fish caught with dolphins in their school cafeteria. Federal law required dolphin protection by American fishermen but not by foreign fishermen. Though the Washington-based Humane Society had sponsored a tuna boycott for fourteen years, it was the students' boycott that immediately moved tuna producers to expand dolphin-safe fishing techniques to their international fishing operations and develop the dolphin-safe label on their tuna cans. No doubt this quick action spared the tuna industry a national boycott and the fate of Perrier, Audi, helium balloons, and others.[15]

After children in terms of their media power come animals. The Concerned Ladies of the Everglades used a letter "written" by Chief, a golden retriever, to the Bushs' dog Millie, to get both White House attention and press coverage for Everglades water quality issues.[16]

The next generation is being taught environmentalism from grade school on. Jim Lukaszewski, the leading expert on managing environmental issues, loves to tell the story of a grandfather being instructed by his granddaughter on the proper use of a sink. It seems the grandfather ran the hot water while shaving. His granddaughter reached up to turn off the hot water, telling him, "Grandpa, you can't do that any more. You are hurting the planet." Lukaszewski's workshops and publications built around the theme of "It Ain't Easy Being Green: Communicating Corporate Environmentalism" are packed with valuable issues management insights, strategies, concepts, and humor.[17]

The art and science of defining and forming issue groups are becoming increasingly well established, but at the same time they remain to some degree problematic. In any event, the formation of an issue group is a key step in the life cycle of an issue.

Media Recognition. If an issue is to have any significant impact, it must successfully complete the equivalent of the metamorphosis of an obscure, drab caterpillar crawling in the shadows, into a beautiful butterfly, bursting into the sunlight on iridescent wings. The advocates of every issue dream of this transformation, but few achieve it. While the sky may seem to be filled with butterflies, for every butterfly a hundred or a thousand or more caterpillars lie in waiting. Since virtually every issue born in the last thirty years is still alive, except for Vietnam and Watergate, there is little room for new issues (see Chapter 10).

The issues that do rise to prominence seem to have some common characteristics:

- good visuals—something people can see on TV
- immediacy, clarity of impact
- clearly defined players—victims and villains
- articulate, available spokespersons
- good geography—easily accessible by major networks
- confirmation of existing attitudes or beliefs
- universality—it applies to everybody
- randomness—it could happen to anybody

- unforeseeable—the victims couldn't avoid it
- foreseeability—villains knew or should have known
- availability of low impact, preventive solution

Inflation, an important issue in every economy, has no visuals. CBS tried with its "market basket" of groceries but did not succeed. The terrible costs of a failing education system, teenage pregnancy, and drug abuse also have poor visuals. Since it takes years for the costs to be realized, nothing sufficiently newsworthy happens on any particular day.

While there are many areas with hazardous waste problems, some (like the Valley of the Drums in Kentucky) much worse than Love Canal, none had one of the advantages of this upstate community: it is less than an hour by air from the headquarters of the three TV networks in New York. While local stations increasingly feed to the national networks via satellite links, in the late 1970s when this story broke, getting a national correspondent to the scene for the continuing developments was important. With the broad cuts in network and local news departments, geography may again become important. Love Canal with its innocent homeowner became the symbol for hazardous wastes. While homebuyers are accustomed to structural and termite examinations, none ever thought about digging up the yard to look for buried hazardous wastes. This has become a much broader issue under new EPA regulations, which place the burden of cleanup on the property owner. At least one S&L faced bankruptcy after it foreclosed on a failed shopping center with unknown wastes only to be served with a cleanup bill greater than its assets.

The national TV networks are not the only path by which issues break into the national consciousness, only the fastest. The emergence in the 1960s of programs designed specifically to confront issues, such as *60 Minutes,* offered an alternative to the evening news. Talk shows and TV magazines offer additional paths. The *Koppel Report* and *McNeil/Lehrer* look at fewer issues with greater depth. The birth of Cable News Network (CNN), with hours to fill and refill, has brought many local stories to national prominence. Radio plays a role with call-in shows and programs like *All Things Considered,* where anything might pop up. National news magazines, specialized publications, suburban newspapers, and other print media, all serve to identify issues that may then reach larger audiences through broadcast media.

Once issues have achieved national recognition, the next step is the determination of which of the several institutions will recognize and address the issue—the national legislature; the courts; the executive; the state or local governments; the regulatory bodies; the court of public opinion; or various private mechanisms, negotiations, and agreements. Increasingly, today's executives are able to anticipate issues early enough in the development process and respond quickly and effectively enough to forestall their movement up the public agenda and graduation into major public issues. Thus a

Figure 2.2
Development Cycle of Public Issues

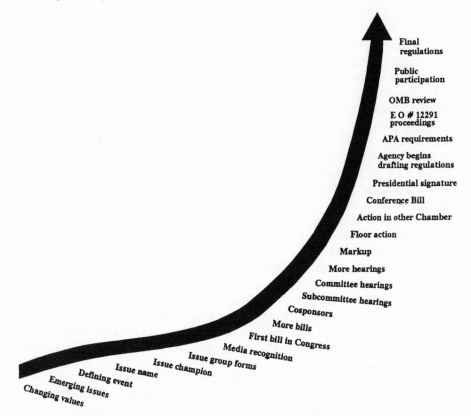

manufacturer issues its own recall before government orders one. In one case, the recall was issued even before any government body knew of the potential problem. The pharmaceutical manufacturers developed tamper-resistant packaging before the government could even draft proposed regulations. Food companies, recognizing their risks of becoming a copycat issue, quickly followed. The development cycle of public issues given in Figure 2.2 shows the path to government regulations open to issues not resolved by preemptive, proactive means.

Perhaps the success of such issues management programs explains why the list of major U.S. social protection legislation ends in 1980 and issues activists—frustrated in their inability to make and move any new issue—have turned to old ones. First the old "ban the bomb" movement was recycled as the nuclear freeze issue, then South Africa became a rallying point, and finally Dan Quayle became the butt of countless jokes. Forgotten for two decades, university "support" for South Africa through accounts in banks with South African correspondent branches and investments also returned. This was one of the first issues over which students staged "sit-ins" at university offices back in the 1960s.

The lack of movement of issues at the national level and the continued proactive response to emerging issues gave rise to several developments. First, many advocates turned to the states with their issues. Unable to get a national ban on pop-top cans or legislation requiring deposits for disposable containers, for example, environmentalists took their issue to the states. Second, a new class of issues emerged: national–local issues—those with national standing but local resolution. Drunk driving is perhaps the most prominent example.

Issues that do not evolve through the early stages have little opportunity for any significant resolution. Immediately after the 1980 election, the "nuclear freeze" issue "emerged." This was clearly a new kind of issue with none of the traditional roots of a genuine national issue: no defining event (no book, no happening, etc.); no issue champion; no basis in changed or reinterpreted societal values; no real or imagined constituency; no confirmation of preexisting attitudes or beliefs. Nevertheless, it did generate a stampede of more than 258 freeze bills in Congress—none of which ever saw the light of day.

The true nature of the freeze issue was exposed in a masterfully orchestrated power play by ABC Television in its November 1983 made-for-TV movie, *The Day After*. Not only did ABC hoodwink the entire antiestablishment freeze movement (including some very establishment religious institutions) into actively and aggressively promoting its viewership, ABC also hoodwinked the White House, which made everybody but the president (from secretaries of state and defense on down) available for a national town meeting immediately following the show. ABC achieved its McLuhanesque goal: the whole world was watching. This nonissue nevertheless immediately disappeared when ratings week ended. ABC used every major institution in the society through this nonissue to boost its ratings. Fortunately, the ratings were not high enough, and according to a popular joke from a skit on NBC's irreverent *Saturday Night Live,* many lives were saved. ABC was set to run a series and nuke twenty cities the next season if the ratings were high enough.

The nuclear freeze issue had everything going for it—media attention, professional champions, celebrities, events (350,000 attended a free nuclear freeze concert in Central Park) issue groups, supporting legislation; but having no real base, it disappeared even faster than it appeared.

The South Africa issue is in a different class. Just as the new private constitution represents a carryover of democratic political concepts into the private sector with no appreciation of the boundaries between them, so it is with the South Africa issue. When the National Collegiate Athletic Association (NCAA) announced it would require drug tests, student athletes complained about violations of their Sixth Amendment protections from unreasonable search and seizure. When the Pope removed Father Curran from the faculty of Catholic University for challenging church doctrine, his defenders decried the infringement of his First Amendment right of free speech. That the U.S. Constitution does not mention the NCAA, the Catholic Church, or other governments and institutions is no matter. Legal scholars and commentators may view such extraordinary interpretations of the Bill of Rights as naive and the courts may not accept tortuous arguments expanding the scope of government involvement and the courts' jurisdiction over these institutions. However, such intellectual niceties on the part of the existing order duck the fundamental nature of the challenge. If these institutions are now as powerful over the individual as the frail government was in 1789 when the Bill of Rights was written, then these basic rights should now constrain these new institutions. The American penchant for fairness virtually requires that they do.

Without a doubt, the emerging private sector constitution will ultimately contain a bill of rights as revolutionary for these times as the original bill was in 1789. As logic, reason, and the courts reach the limits of expanding the authority of government in projecting basic political rights into the private sector, it is only reasonable to expect that some other mechanism will be found to carry these rights into new institutions.[18]

In the private sector, it is a new de facto constitution. In international affairs, it is human rights. Traditional paradigms, boundaries, structures, and institutions will not survive the challenge presented by this change in values.

The model of the development process of issues is based on historical analogy and a basic human characteristic. The first impression is a lasting one. While this has long been clear for human relations, it has also emerged as a principle of issues management, albeit in a modified form:

Those who define the issue win the debate.

Because most of the issues that have had tremendous impact on corporations have been defined by outside participants, corporations initially focused on their only option — responding and reacting to issues already defined — usually with little more effect than minor damage control. Though this function is necessary and will continue, issues management adds an emphasis on corporate involvement in the issues-defining process. Where an issue is already defined, it may become necessary to

Redefine the issue to win a new debate.

Having little chance to prevail over their competition on the issues of quality and economy, American car manufacturers now emphasize their better safety records — the very nemesis that forced the new paradigm on them in the first place.

The importance of defining the issue is based on a phenomenon of public issues:

Opinion is fact.

Logic, reason, and even solid scientific proof to the contrary, what a person believes to be fact is for all practical matters, indeed fact for that person and his or her decisions. This is especially so where the complexity of issues supports a variety of opinions among the experts and the fabled "reasonable men" can and do disagree—noisily and in public. The issue of nuclear power, for example, demands so much prominence in the minds of some people because for them nuclear power is dangerous. No statistics on probability, no logic, no reasoning, and no endless reminders that not even one person has ever been killed by nuclear power in the United States will change their opinion.

Issues with long-term uncertain impacts or with impacts that cannot be proven beyond any challenge, issues with the appearance of the potential of the possibility of danger (notwithstanding safety measures), or issues involving risks down to one in a billion billion (one is still one) are all subject to strong public opinion reactions if they are defined in an unbalanced manner. Many more people have died in mining coal, drilling for oil, or transporting these bulky fuels. Moreover, these fuels raise serious environmental problems, from acid rain to damage to the ozone layer to the greenhouse effect. Any rational tradeoff would take the nuclear option. But the sensationalism of the nuclear risk prevails.

On Long Island, New York's Governor Cuomo, a politician who made a career out of acid rain, wants to disassemble a $6-billion nuclear power plant. One good story about a person killed by a seat belt—10 percent of the time, as noted earlier, a motorist would be better off without a belt—could overturn the national policy requiring seat belt use.

Similarly, for the prisoner furlough program, the statistics show that society is well served by this program, though a very small number—fewer than 3 percent—abuse the program. Repeat crimes by ex-convicts after release are much less frequent among those whose transition into the community has been facilitated by the furlough program. However, after one widely reported assault and rape in Maryland by a furloughed prisoner from Massachusetts, Governor Dukakis suspended the entire program.

This rape by Willie Horton became a major campaign issue in the 1988 presidential election because Horton was serving a sentence of life without parole when he was furloughed. The Massachusetts legislature had passed a bill expressly prohibiting those who were never scheduled for release into society to be in the program designed for their transition back into society. Since Massachusetts has no death penalty, it has no greater punishment it can apply to a Willie Horton for additional crimes. Governor Dukakis had vetoed the bill.

Given the public's appetite for the sensational — some people always stop to gawk at a highway carnage — and the media's frantic competition to satisfy this appetite, the incentives all promote the development and presentation of the most unbalanced definitions of issues. However mistaken — or misled by itself or others — public opinion may be, it becomes as important as fact since such "fact" will guide public behavior. Since with issues as with people the first impression is so lasting, it is usually more efficient to direct efforts to redefining an issue than to contesting it. Because this option is not always available or feasible within reasonable allocations of resources, early warning and participation in defining an issue is essential.

RECYCLED ISSUES

No sooner did the life cycle model of major national issues gain recognition, use, and general acceptance than the issues process evolved, requiring adjustments, revisions, and alternatives. Foremost among these was the phenomenon of recycled issues — issues that had been all the way through the issues process, passing out of the Congress and through the regulatory phases only to return again. For some issues, Yogi Berra was only too close to the mark:

It ain't over 'till it's over.

Except for Vietnam and Watergate, it ain't over yet for virtually every major national issue born since the emergence of the national news media created a national (and later global) village.

For the most part, these were horizontal social issues and their attendant regulations — cutting across all industries and sectors of the economy — as distinguished from the more traditional, vertical economic regulations that focused on a single industry. Too often, Congress found these broader, horizontal social laws were more complex than was first recognized. Too often, legislation was based on insufficient policy research and analysis. A key requirement in the first Clean Air Act, for example, turned out to be unknowingly based on data taken on an unusually hot summer day in Denver, the Mile-High City — hardly the best basis for setting national standards.

Since the horizontal social regulations — environmental regulations, worker safety laws, pension reforms, and the like — applied to all industries, no single industry felt the need to participate in drafting the enabling legislation. Yet when confronted with the specific regulations, industries really began to feel the pinch.

Since there was little flexibility at the regulatory level, they brought issues back to the Congress, with the common theme: "The rules are too strict, the standards, too high. We can't live with them. Congress must tone them

Figure 2.3
Recycled Issues: Model 2

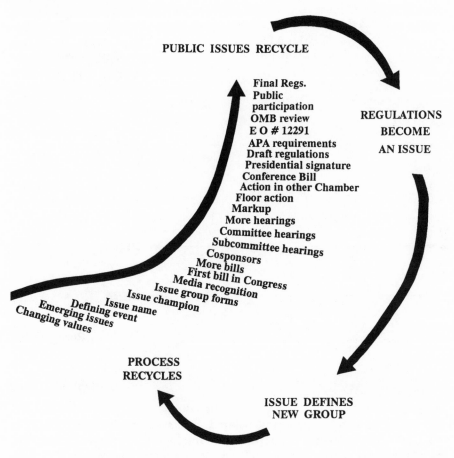

PUBLIC ISSUES RECYCLE

Final Regs.
Public
participation
OMB review
E O # 12291
APA requirements
Draft regulations
Presidential signature
Conference Bill
Action in other Chamber
Floor action
Markup
More hearings
Committee hearings
Subcommittee hearings
Cosponsors
More bills
First bill in Congress
Media recognition
Issue group forms
Issue champion
Issue name
Defining event
Emerging issues
Changing values

REGULATIONS
BECOME
AN ISSUE

PROCESS
RECYCLES

ISSUE DEFINES
NEW GROUP

down. It must back off." The effect of this "back off" cry was to recycle issues, as shown in Figure 2.3.

The back-off cry was not limited to industry but included virtually every group facing the new standards. It was the mayors of New York, Chicago, and Los Angeles who brought the ambient air quality issue back to Congress. It seems they could not meet the standards in their cities and faced the loss of their transportation subsidies if they did not. Congress finally did back off the standards. And for the most part, after dodging the point with deregulation for several years, Congress did back off elsewhere, postponing, reducing, or otherwise mitigating the impact of the horizontal social laws it had so hastily enacted earlier. Mileage and emission standards for automobiles,

Figure 2.4
Vertical and Horizontal Regulations

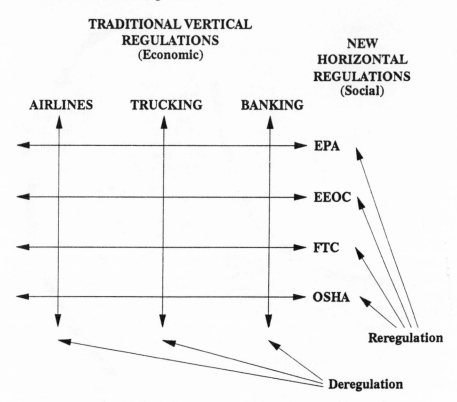

for example, were reduced and delayed. The seat belt–ignition interlocks required on 1974 cars were dropped. So were a host of EPA standards. Safety standards were adjusted for efficiency. OSHA's 400-page proposed ruling on the proper use of stepladders was never issued after it drew congressional fire.

The distinction between vertical economic regulation and horizontal deregulation is shown in Figure 2.4. When industry complained about excessive horizontal social legislation, Congress tried to satisfy industry without offending advocates of horizontal regulation by pressing for deregulation of specific vertical industries. Though this was hardly responsive, it gave the appearance of being responsive and bought needed political space for members of Congress caught between the original advocates and those recycling the issue for softened standards.

Backing off was not an easy task for either the Congress or regulatory agencies. Often when regulatory agencies had a new law to enforce, they turned to the Congress for the needed staff expertise to draft and administer new regulations. Having worked for the passage of the enabling legislation, these congressional staff knew the law, but often they had also become advocates of the standards and goals. Policy wars over backing off broke out between the old guard ideologues at the agencies and the new pragmatists in Congress. Congress had to shut down the Federal Trade Commission no less than three times to bring its regulatory excesses under control. While the FTC was an extreme example, the back-off process pitted the agencies and the special interest groups who wanted the higher standards against both the Congress and those who had to live by the higher standards. Congress became less of a legislating institution and more of a relegislating one.

A good example of the relegislating process is the reauthorization of the Clean Air Act in the 101st Congress. Rep. John Dingel (D–Michigan) guided the drafting of this monster—so large it took four staff members to carry it to the House floor. This bill became a bit of an embarrassment when it was discovered that it contained $19 million to study the effect of methane from the flatulence of cows on the ozone layer. Though these funds were expressly removed in both the House and Senate, and therefore could not be restored at the conference stage (and there is no record they were), when the bill was finally passed, somebody, presumably staff, had reinserted the $19 million. Clearly, no one in the House or Senate knew what was in the monster they passed. Moreover, the first thing the environmental group awarded these "research" funds did was prepare a video news release (VNR) defending this absurd waste of federal funds.[19]

THE CONGRESSIONAL BYPASS

With trench warfare raging over old, recycled issues, new issues could not get through Congress. Those who sought to advance their issues turned to other forums. While much was made of the Reagan Revolution's return of power to the states, a much more important force was the necessity for the states to act because Congress could not. Thus Texas passed legislation for its Vietnam veterans exposed to agent orange—hardly a state issue. Oregon led the way on environmental issues, passing the first bottle bill to require deposits on beverage containers, while Florida pioneered in issues of the privacy of patient medical records. Responding to a variety of women's issues, the EEOC decided—without specific additional legislation from Congress—that its broad mandate to fight discrimination included sexual discrimination. A host of other groups seeking to move their issues turned to the courts. All these institutions were used to bypass the stalemated Congress, as shown in Figure 2.5.

THE LEGISLATIVE AGENDA OF THE CONGRESS

With the issue of recycling continuing and the bypass in full swing, major pieces of legislation have become stuck in Congress. According to the Con-

Figure 2.5
Congressional Bypass

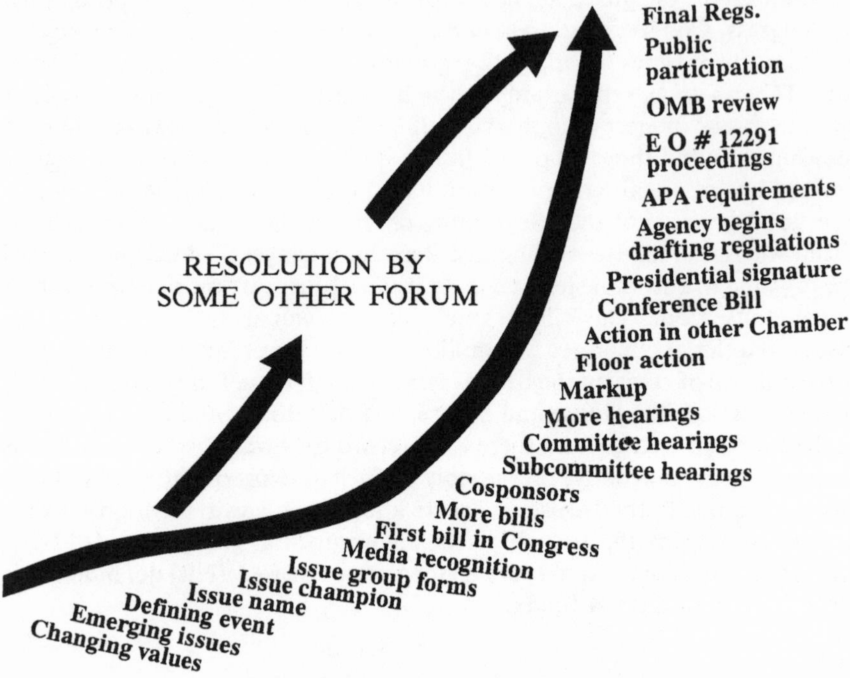

Final Regs.

Public
participation

OMB review

E O # 12291
proceedings

APA requirements

Agency begins
drafting regulations

Presidential signature

Conference Bill

Action in other Chamber

Floor action

Markup

More hearings

Committee hearings

Subcommittee hearings

Cosponsors

More bills

First bill in Congress

Media recognition

Issue group forms

Issue champion

Issue name

Defining event

Emerging issues

Changing values

RESOLUTION BY
SOME OTHER FORUM

gressional Research Service, the last of the horizontal social laws enacted was Superfund, passed in 1980. Congress has not gone out of the legislating business but changed the way it passes legislation. One of the major reforms of the late 1970s was the concept of *sunset legislation*—the idea that every law, program, and authorization should have a "sunset," a certain date when it would expire unless specifically extended by Congress.

The calendar of expiring programs, authorizations, and laws has become de facto the new legislative agenda for the Congress. This calendar sets the dates by which renewal legislation must be passed. Unlike other legislation which can be (and is) always delayed, legislation to prevent sunset must be passed before the deadline, or the program, agency, authorization, or law expires. In such a case, the only activity its employees are authorized to undertake is shutting down.

With the original advocates of a sunsetting program still in town, with its legislative sponsors, committees, and subcommittees still in place, as well as those now benefitting from the program, it is a virtual certainty that a bill authorizing at a minimum an extension of the sunset deadline will be presented and passed in both houses of Congress. With this "iron triangle" of advocates and beneficiaries, government agencies with jobs at stake, and legislators with vested interests, congressional action is pro forma.

As a renewal bill comes to the floor, there is of course an opportunity for mischief through the attachment of an amendment or two. Only the loose rule that amendments must be germane to the bill limits the games, and such mischief has caused a major perversion of the legislative process. Since most of the legislation of Congress cannot get through the blocked channels of the traditional process, it is now passed by this back-door, piecemeal process without the deliberative, comprehensive legislative stages of subcommittee and committee hearings, mark-up, debate, and the like. One bill in the 100th Congress had more than ninety floor amendments added in a wild eleventh-hour frenzy. Some of these last-minute amendments were in direct conflict with one another, reflecting little (if any) coherent policy to the agencies that were required to draft the necessary implementing regulations and providing scarcely a hint of "congressional intent" to guide interpretations by the courts.

Analysts at the Congressional Research Service estimate that as much as 35 percent of the original content of the acid rain legislation was passed via the sunset agenda before any acid rain bill was passed. In early April 1989, housing activists got an amendment attached to a housing reauthorization bill to prohibit condominiums and retirement communities from barring owners with minor children. Opponents of the ban read about it in the paper two days later.[20]

Under the sunset principle, each new Congress faces a long list of laws, programs, and authorizations that must be reviewed and renewed by particular dates during one of its two sessions. Figure 2.6 shows how many sunset reviews were already on the agenda at the beginning of the 102nd and 103rd Congresses. The difference between the two lines shows the sunset reviews in the 102nd Congress that were completed and then placed on the agendas of subsequent Congresses.[21] Obviously, the most popular was a "one Congress" (two-year) extension—the 103rd Congress began with more than 1,000 reviews on the agenda of its first session. There are already items on the agenda of Congresses fifteen years in the future.

The traditional legislative process of drafting new legislation, with proponents and opponents fighting over each word, is like traditional warfare, sometimes even trench warfare. Each side amasses its forces for the great conflict, which has bounds and rules not unlike those propounded by the Marquis of Queensberry.

If this is traditional warfare, the sunset agenda is the antithesis; this is legislative terrorism. The rule is that there are no rules; anything goes. Under the sunset agenda, the legislative process has become one of hit-and-run guerrilla terrorism tactics requiring every group, industry, agency, association, and profession to maintain a complete police, intelligence, and security

Figure 2.6
Legislative Terrorism: Legislation by Sunset Amendment

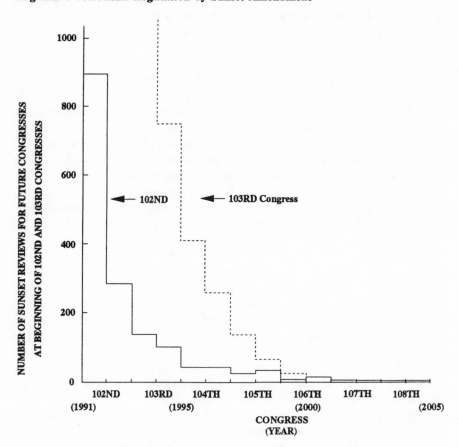

force with continuous vigilance and a rapid-response capability prepared to counter a legislative-terrorist strike in the dead of night.

This has been a boom to the insiders of Washington and created a market for computerized legislative tracking services. It is, however, hardly any way to make public policy. The hearing process, once used to develop legislation, is now primarily a source of media coverage for congressmen. Hearings are "staged" for C-span and CNN, usually with a movie or rock star testifying as an "expert" to assure a good turnout and good ratings. Such a reformed legislative process contains a certain element of both comedy and tragedy. It is probably important to remember that the ideas that led to legislative terrorism began as well-intended reforms. For a discussion on the demise of the legislative process and the collapse of Congress as a national forum for the resolution of public issues, see Chapter 10.

In 1985, the Edison Electric Institute launched a study of models of the public issues process. Under the direction of Gerald Edgly, Joe Coates, an independent contractor, studied three models: the pre-cursor jurisdiction model with Graham T. T. Molitor as its leading proponent, a technology-driven model by R. T. Lawless, and the first model outlined earlier.[22]

NATIONAL–LOCAL ISSUES

The inability of Congress to move any major issues forward through the legislative process has caused no small amount of frustration among those advocating specific resolutions to issues. With the path to federal legislation blocked, advocates have turned elsewhere. The search for alternatives has included the courts, professional associations, quasi-legislative bodies, and rule-making agencies, as well as state and local legislative bodies. The drunk driving issue, as noted earlier, is a national issue that has virtually all its attention focused on the local level. While the Twenty-first Amendment to the Constitution gives the states absolute authority to control the sale of alcohol, the federal government has many policy options that could be and have been exercised. The federal government used the threat of withholding highway trust funds, for example, to force states to raise the drinking age to twenty-one. However, it has let the states take the lead.

On the comparable-worth issue, clearly a national issue, the Congress has ducked the issue, leaving it to a few brave states to blaze the trail. Similarly, bills requiring deposits for throwaway containers have languished in Congress while some states forged ahead, addressing several problems at once — crowded landfills, litter, recycling, pollution, jobs, and others.

In yet another example of the power of the private sector constitution relative to the traditional public sector constitution, the McDonalds food chain announced in April 1991 that it would stop using polystyrene packaging and use, to the extent practical, recyclable paper products. McDonalds estimates that this will reduce its worldwide contribution to solid wastes by more than 181 million tons annually. While the debate about polystyrene continues in the traditional political arena, McDonalds has anticipated this issue and responded. At the same time, McDonalds also introduced its "McLean" hamburger, responding again ahead of the cycle of the political process on this key health and nutrition issue.

ISSUES AT THE STATE LEVEL

In contrast to the development of national issues through the legislative process in Congress, issues at the state level move along paths that seem almost totally random. Where the building of legislative support is a slow, methodical process, taken step by step, the development of issues among the states seems unforeseeable, not unlike heating fifty kernels of popcorn with issues "popping" unpredictably among the various states.[23]

This image of issues viewed across the space of the fifty states contrasts

Figure 2.7
Forecasting State Legislative Change

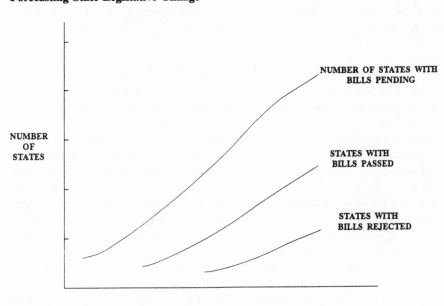

with issues in the Congress viewed across time. While it is possible to track issues across time within a single state, most state legislatures meet during only part of the year, some for only a matter of weeks. During this brief time, a bill addressing an issue either makes it into law or dies. The long, involved congressional process of legislative research and hearings is shrunk to the bare minimum. Like mayflies that live only a day, proposed state legislation lasts only one brief session. Few bills have sufficient momentum to survive a recess and be revived in a subsequent session.

To anticipate the movement of issues among the states, a trend line is generated from the records of states that have considered an issue. Of these, those states that have passed a bill and those that have not are recorded. Since failure to pass a bill is not as fatal for the future as voting it down, this distinction is sometimes made. Since 1978, for example, bills requiring deposits on nonreturnable bottles, so-called bottle bills, have been considered in thirty-one states, adopted in fourteen, rejected in nine, and allowed to die without action in eight others. The trend lines of issues among the states is shown in Figure 2.7.

From historical data such as these, reasonably reliable forecasts of future state actions can be prepared, even though it may be nearly impossible to forecast an outcome in any single state. A more detailed picture of the future of issues among the states can be developed by a more sophisticated analysis of the states involved. It would be helpful if there were one or two bellwether states whose actions would forecast the resolution of issues among other states.

While there are bellwether states for the various kinds of issues — environmental, law enforcement, drugs, and the like — no states are bellwethers on all kinds of issues. Oregon, Minnesota, and Massachusetts have pioneered virtually all state environmental initiatives. Florida has pioneered the privacy of medical records. California and New York have pioneered innovations in public administration. Tennessee, home of many pharmaceutical manufacturing plants, passed the first copycat drug law, making it illegal to counterfeit prescription tranquilizers and other legal drugs.

Though bellwether states remain a valuable refinement of the state popcorn model, surprises are still possible. Iowa, for example, was the first state to require employers to provide bilingual supervisors if they have ten or more workers for whom English is a second language. Heretofore, Iowa was not recognized as a bellwether state for employment issues.

Two other mechanisms can disturb the popcorn model. If an issue appears suddenly and has sufficient immediacy, a state legislature may simply copy the legislation passed by another state without even taking time to particularize it to its own circumstances. Such copycat legislation can sweep through the states quickly with little warning, as legislation on assault rifles did in 1989.

A somewhat slower but still rapid change is the phenomenon of policy crossover. When a new public policy has been developed to address a particular issue, it may be applied suddenly to a companion issue without undergoing much, if any, legislative development. New York state, for example, struggled with the concept of requiring electric utilities to provide minimum service at minimum rates so that the elderly and infirm would not suffer in the harsh upstate winters. It took months of public debate and legislative staff work to get a "lifeline" bill through. After it was all done, it occurred to some legislators that the same people also need minimum telephone service to call for medical services in an emergency. Without so much a "by your leave, sir" to the phone companies, the legislature picked up the lifeline policy and applied it to telephone service.

During the 1980s, commercial firms began to provide electronic tracking services focused on the states. These services, modeled on those covering federal legislation, allowed interested parties anywhere in the country to track developments among the states. As a result, a bill introduced in any state rings like a call to arms across the country to those involved in the issues addressed. This is extremely important for national–local issues or issues blocked in Congress that are being taken for the first time to the states where advocates of one position or another are trying to demonstrate support and momentum.

As with every system mankind has built, the first development is a method for defeating the system. Clever issue advocates have learned that the introduction of a bill serves as an early warning of impending action to their opponents across the country via computerized tracking services. They also know that a summary of the content of each bill will be prepared only once, with amendments appearing by title, if at all, later. An innocuous bill on a related minor or strictly local topic will slip by the computerized watchdogs. Once a bill has been entered in the computerized state reporting systems, an amendment can be added, or a complete substitute bill entered, without much or any notice from the reporting services. An innocuous bill can be turned into a raging tiger without alerting the national network of the opposition. This is an example of legislative terrorism on the state level. As with sunset terrorism, the only limit to the game is a state's enforcement of its germaneness rules on the amendments and substitutions—the same limits that moderate legislative terrorism at the congressional level.

In addition to monitoring them with high-speed computerized services, states can be tracked through one or more of their own organizations. The Council of State Policy and Planning Agencies runs a state scanning program. The National Conference of State Legislators has a newsletter on state issues and prepares issue briefs on state issues. The Council of State Government publishes what for many state legislators is the bible of state legislation. Entitled simply, *Suggested State Legislation,* this book contains model state legislation on a wide variety of current state topics. Moreover, knowing when a model bill was published serves to map early developments leading to the current status quo. This list of previous sample bills is presented in each annual edition.[24]

The final model of the development cycle of public issues, shown in Figure 2.8, includes the internal congressional bypass of the legislative agenda, as well as the external bypass of the states, the courts, and the regulatory agencies. This final model is still working within the paradigm of the existing social contract—the U.S. Constitution. It will need to be adapted to include the new private sector constitution.

THE LIMITS OF MODELS

By the early 1980s, it became clear that the setting, context, level, nature, and, most important, immediate environment of an issue—the status and future of other issues before, beside, and behind that issue—are factors as important to how and why the issue emerges as the issue itself—possibly more important. Specifically, the original factors identified for major national issues must be redefined, depending on the different environments in which those issues emerge—whether they are global, national, state or local, for example, or product, corporation, or industry; or social, technical, economic,

Figure 2.8
Summary: Development Cycle of Issues

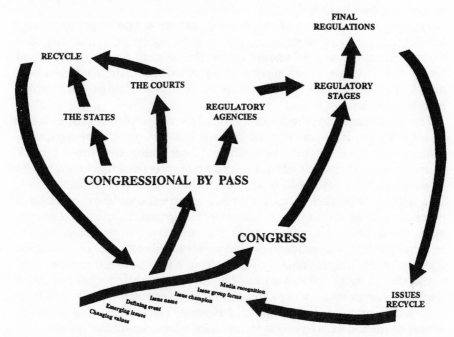

or legislative. They can also be internal or external, direct or indirect, immediate or delayed, and so on.

The issue of nuclear weapons plants went nowhere as long as it was confined to the context of a series of many other local issues. It was not until it touched on national security that it moved to the national agenda. Love Canal became a symbol of toxic wastes, though several other sites were both larger and more dangerous (for instance, the town of Times Beach in Missouri and the Valley of the Drums in Kentucky).

Moreover, all these factors shaping the emergence of issues are rapidly changing as the technology of the public issues process changes and as more players learn how to use the new technologies. As a result, even identical issues a few months apart do not fit the same model.

It becomes clear for this level of sophistication and pace of technological change that each issue is rapidly becoming unique, requiring its own "model." It must also be clear that it is time to take another perspective, to develop another paradigm of the issues process. The earlier paradigm that models could describe the development of issues is based on looking at each issue in isolation. The perspective was a sequential one of "issue after issue" following a path. Today, the issue agenda is so congested that issues are all moving—or, more precisely, not moving—in simultaneous lock step, a gridlock of bumper-car-like jostling.[25]

The major determinants of the course of an issue are no longer its characteristics measured against some objective criteria describing a path but rather the movement of the surrounding issues. Rather than a paradigm focused on models of single issues moving along in isolation, the paradigm now must be the flow (or lack of flow) of the whole stream of issues within which each issue of interest moves.

The role of technology in the evolution of the congressional process is one of some debate. It may be just coincidence that during the computerization of the bill drafting, legislative research, and floor voting, the process became so established that models of the public issues process described above could be developed, linking public issues directly with legislative issues.

In spite of (or perhaps because of) the computerization of the congressional process, so many errors were made in legislating that recycling and relegislating issues grew to dominance. At the same time, notwithstanding the tremendous growth in productivity due to advanced computer technologies, the number of congressional staff grew from a few thousand to more than twenty-five thousand. It can certainly be argued that the network legislative tracking systems such as Legislate and ELIS (Electronic Legislative Information Service) have greatly expanded awareness of and participation in the details of the legislative process to the point where the traditional development process of hearings, mark-up, committee report, and floor action is stymied—leaving only the hit-and-run guerrilla tactics of the legislative agenda created by the sunset calendar.

This leaves the people in a curious position: the institution they traditionally rely on to restore their sense of balance when technology disturbs them cannot function because the technology got there first, disturbing that institution itself. While technology surges onward, they are left to ponder: how do the people fix a broken fixer?

This is not just a problem of the legislative process. The political implications of congressional information technology—primarily the relatively low technology of computerized mass mailings to constituents—means that during the 1980s the replacement of legislators in a system with free, two-party elections in the United States is less than turnover in the closed, one-party elections for Russia's Supreme Soviet, which resulted almost entirely from the advanced age of the members of this body. No wonder *The New York Times* editorialized on the "Need for House Repair" and the *Washington Post's* David Broder asked, "How about a Little Glasnost for the House?"[26] The scandals focused on alleged violations and improper conduct by current and former House members and senators are a distraction from the real issue: the real scandal is not the violations but the incredible conduct allowed by the "ethics" rules enacted by Congress. This is one emerging issue that will not bypass the Congress.

Two other aspects of models limit their value. First, it is not clear, as an issue is developing, which of the models will apply to its particular situation. In hindsight an issue may fit a model sufficiently well, but the real value of models lies in their forecasting role. The situation is not one of chaos, but it is evolving in that direction. Most issues still start with the traditional development cycle. Only after Congress has failed to act is one of the alternatives likely to be explored—the sunset agenda, the states, the courts, or regulatory agencies. However, the continued necessity of eventually having to use one of the alternate paths will mean that Congress will not even get to review an issue that is taken immediately to a more responsive forum. While history provides some guidance about which issues are likely to be taken to which forums, the reliability of this guidance is fading.

A second problem is inherent to the two major models of congressional action: using the traditional model, the content of legislation can be anticipated, but the timing cannot; under the sunset model, the timing is well known, but the content is not. These models forecast either what or when, but not both. This is a sociopolitical version of the Hiesenberg Uncertainty Principle of nuclear physics which holds that there is an absolute limit to how much can be known—nature has a built-in degree of uncertainty that cannot be removed.[27] This natural uncertainty has grown into the most complex systems of mankind—the process of writing the rules by which mankind lives.

When he was offered the mostly ceremonial post of President of the new state of Israel, Albert Einstein declined, observing

> Physics is simple, politics is complex;
> physics is eternal, politics is temporal.

3

The Link to Strategic Planning

If we could better understand where we are and where we are tending,
we could better determine where we want to go and how to get there.
— Lincoln

The prime tasks of strategic management are to understand the current and future operating environment, define organizational mission and goals, identify options, evaluate and implement strageies to achieve the mission and goals, and evaluate actual performance — to lead the organization with a vision of the future. Thus, as Peter Drucker observes, strategic planning exploits the new and different opportunities of tomorrow, in contrast to long-range planning, which tries to optimize for tomorrow the trends of today.[1]

More than a century ago, Lincoln laid out the four stages of traditional long-range planning from the perspective of a stable external world with the planning focus on internal issues. Whitehead's 1931 observation, noted in Chapter 1, says what everyone now accepts: the pace of change no longer tolerates an assumption of a stable external world. The long-range perspective must include the changing externalities.

THE STRATEGIC PLANNING PROCESS

Although most organizations currently do long-range planning, many have found they can fruitfully augment this work with strategic planning concepts and enhance their ability to steer a course in a changing external environment. In this section, the traditional long-range planning and envi-

Figure 3.1
The Internal Perspective

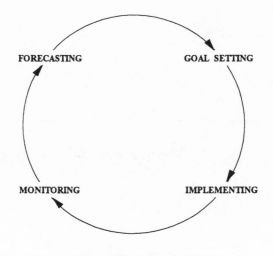

FORECASTING   GOAL SETTING

MONITORING   IMPLEMENTING

LONG RANGE PLANNING

ronmental-scanning models are briefly described and then merged to provide the basis of a strategic planning process.

Traditional long-range planning in its elementary form is based on *at least* the four key steps Lincoln identified. The four steps address these questions: (1) Where is the organization now? (2) Where is it going (or tending)? (3) Where does it want to go? and (4) What does it have to do to change where it is going to get where it wants to go? The steps required to answer these four questions are monitoring, forecasting, goal-setting, and implementing.[2]

Performing these activities is a continuing process that, for example, produces a one-year operating plan and a five- or ten-year long-range plan every year. The long-range planning cycle begins by monitoring selected trends of interest to the organization, forecasting the expected future of those trends (usually based upon extrapolation from historical data using regression analysis or other curve-fitting techniques), defining the desired future by setting organizational goals in the context of the expected future, developing and implementing specific policies and actions designed to reduce the differences between the expected future and the desired future, and monitoring the effects of these actions and policies on the selected trends (see Figure 3.1).

The environmental scanning model of the external perspective (Figure 3.2) begins with scanning the external environment for emerging issues that pose threats or opportunities to the organization. As part of this step, trends are

Figure 3.2
The External Perspective

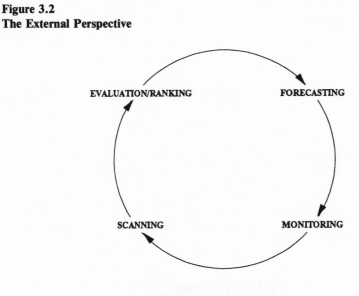

ENVIRONMENTAL SCANNING

specified that define the issues and can be used to measure changes in their nature or significance. Each potential issue or trend is then analyzed in the evaluating or ranking stage to determine the likelihood that it will emerge and the nature and degree of its impact on the organization if it should actually materialize. This stage produces a rank-ordering of the issues and trends according to their importance to current or planned operations.

The next stage, forecasting, focuses on developing an understanding of the expected future for the most important issues and trends. In this stage, any of the modern forecasting techniques may be used. Once the forecasts are made, each of the issues and trends is then monitored to track its continued relevance and to detect any major departures from the forecasts made in the preceding stage. Monitoring, in effect, identifies areas for additional and continued scanning. For example, subsequent monitoring may begin to suggest that a forecast of the employee turnover rate is incorrect. This would imply the need for more focused scanning, forecasting, and analysis to develop a more credible projection.

MERGING INTERNAL AND EXTERNAL PERSPECTIVES

As noted earlier, one of the major limitations of the traditional long-range planning model is that information about the changing external environment is usually not taken into account in a systematic or comprehensive way.

Figure 3.3
The Balanced Perspective

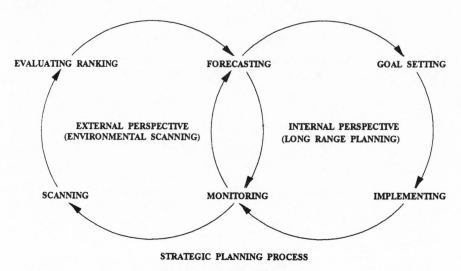

STRATEGIC PLANNING PROCESS

When this omission occurs because of an assumption that "executives cannot predict external changes," long-range planning destines itself to surprise and failure, if only because it locks itself to the information known from direct experience in the past and immediate present.

However, information from the external environment adds important components to long-range planning. First, it identifies new and potentially crucial subjects that should be added to those already identified and tracked in the monitoring stage of the long-range planning model. Second, it identifies possible developments, which must be used to adjust the forecasts of the internal issues derived from forecasting stage. Specifically, these are the surprise events used in Policy Impact Analysis or techniques like Probabilistic System Dynamics, and employed in other rigorous forecasting methods used in the traditional long-range planning process.

These two models of planning, the long-range planning model and the environmental-scanning model, are fundamentally linked. Figure 3.3 shows the balanced perspective of the interrelated model where the strategic planning process consists of six identifiable stages: environmental scanning, evaluation of issues, forecasting, goal setting, implementation, and monitoring. The merged model, then, allows information from the external environment in the form of emerging developments to enter the traditionally inwardly focused planning system, thereby enhancing the overall effectiveness of the corporation's planning process.

The argument for combining these two models can be seen by contrasting two futures: the future that happens to a corporation and the future that happens for it. In the future that happens to a corporation (i.e., the typical "planned" future), new issues are not anticipated before they force their way to the top of the agenda, demanding crisis management and the latest fire-fighting techniques. In this future, issues are usually defined by others whose interests do not necessarily include those of the industry and the corporation or their missions, goals, and purposes. Not only are threats from the external environment not anticipated as early as possible, key opportunities will either be missed or diminished in value.

In the future that happens for the corporation (i.e., the "strategic" future), executive leadership is focused more in the fire-prevention mode, with less need for the fire-fighting mode. Hence it is able to exercise more careful judgment in the orderly and efficient allocation of resources. Certainly, senior executives will still need to deal with unforeseen developments, but these will be fewer in number and less traumatic. Thus, senior management will be able to pursue its mission with greater confidence and consistency as it is interrupted by fewer and smaller fire-fighting exercises.

4

Issues Management: Overview of the Process

The response of an organization to emerging issues in its external environment takes many forms. If issues are not anticipated and identified early in their development life, the response is crisis management on an issue-by-issue basis. While a stand-by crisis management capability is always necessary, it is planned to be just that: a stand-by capability and not one that is used.

Another response to the constant barrage of emerging issues is to build a capability to anticipate potential future crises and steer away from them. This is the issues management process. It is a staff, as opposed to line, function. The senior issues manager is analogous to the treasurer or comptroller, keeping track of the organizations issues rather than its monies. The issues manager "keeps the books" on the organizations issues, both current and emerging.

There are many analogies that might be applied to the internal organizational function that comprises issues management. For one, it is like an intelligence operation focused on a place that cannot be observed directly, except that the "place" is not some hostile country but the future. As in the intelligence community, in the issues management community there is much discussion and debate as to whether an intelligence function should include operations. Given the controversy in the 1970s over intelligence operations, Congress and the president have greatly tightened controls over intelligence operations, requiring explicit authorizations at the highest levels. With the lessons that this history teaches, not to mention common sense, it is clear that an issues management capability should have no standing authorization to do anything about the issues on which it is keeping the books. Just as a treasurer or comptroller is not authorized to spend the organization's resources without strict approval by the highest levels, so it is for the issues manager. At the same time, the issues management team should be prepared to assist whatever actions or operations the authorized leadership directs.

With the focus on the intelligence aspects, issues management consists of at least four, interlocked stages: (1) scanning for emerging issues, (2) researching, analyzing, and forecasting the issues, (3) prioritizing the many issues identified by the scanning and research stages, and (4) developing strategies and issue operation (or action) plans. If the organization leadership decides to undertake an issue operation or action, it may use some, all, or none of the issue management team. Whatever resources are used, an issue operation or action consists of implementing some plan as well as oversight of the operation.

From the perspective of the CEO, issues management includes both intelligence and operations — a total of six stages. From the perspective of everyone below the CEO, it consists of intelligence only. W. Howard Chase is the leading proponent for the first perspective.[1] As Chase operates almost exclusively at this level, where this perspective is applicable, the six stages do apply. This perspective is not, however, one that can be used below this level.

Finally, the division between research and priority setting-stages cannot be nearly as neat as the crisp stages seem to imply: there is a bit of a chicken-and-egg process at work here. The scanning process will identify hundreds, if not thousands, of issues each year that will need to be both researched and prioritized. On the one hand, no organization has the resources to research, analyze, and forecast all the newly identified issues. On the other, emerging issues cannot be evaluated in the priority-setting process unless they have been researched. If the scanning system is working at state-of-the-art levels, it will be identifying issues at such an early stage it will be impossible to anticipate their potential importance without some research, analysis, and forecasting. Obviously, the interlocking nature of these two stages requires that they evolve together.

PART II

Issues Management: The Organizational Process

5

Key Stages of the Issues Management Process

There are two key dimensions to issues management. The first consists of the concepts, process models, and theories of how and why issues move in our society on the various levels — local, state, national, and international — presented in Chapters 1 through 4. These are external, public processes.

A second dimension of issues management is the internal, private organizational process, the implementation and operation of an issues management capability. This is analogous to operating a budget cycle, strategic-planning system, or other management system. Unfortunately, in the literature these two different aspects of issues management have been described in similar, if not identical, terms — issues management processes, models, and so forth. Indeed, the Edison Electric Institute presented its study of what EEI calls the "Lawless, Molitor and Renfro models" of the public issues process in a report entitled, "Models of Issues Management."[1] These are in reality the models of the public issues process used in issues management programs. This chapter addresses the organizational design and operation of systems that make up an organizational response to the public issues process called issues management.

The issues management process has four essential stages:

1. Identifying potential issues by scanning the horizon and beyond of the corporation's current and planned operating environment and peripheral environment

2. Researching the background, future, and potential impacts of these issues

3. Evaluating issues competing for anticipatory operations and action programs

4. Developing strategies for these anticipatory operations

All this information is generated for a purpose—to identify strategies and actions to implement before an issue develops into a crisis. Such actions or operations are not part of the standing mission of an issues management process. See Chapter 4 for a discussion of the necessity of separating the intelligence and operations aspects of issues management.

These different stages are often seen as making up a cycle, usually an annual one timed to the strategic planning cycle. Though usually run in an interlocked cycle, these stages are unique enough to be examined first separately and then in the context of a cycle.

IDENTIFYING EMERGING ISSUES: ENVIRONMENTAL SCANNING

Environmental scanning is usually said to be focused on the external environment. The distinction between external and internal issues is somewhat arbitrary, difficult to define, and in the end unnecessary for scanning purposes. Whether an issue in internal or external depends on how unusual its origin and impact are. Whether the Audi automobile's sudden-acceleration syndrome was internal or external to a corporation's environment depends on how close it was to Audi and to the U.S. luxury car market. Some Audi competitors were concerned enough about being drawn into the issue to add a brake-to-transmission interlock to prevent the possibility of sudden acceleration.

While it is true that much of the driving force in the development of the issues management concept has taken the form of unforeseen issues emerging in the external environment of corporations, a good environmental scanning function is not so focused on external issues as to ignore issues that arise internally and have little or no external dimension—at least at first. For the discussion that follows, then, environmental scanning includes issues or potential issues that could be important to the future of the corporation if they mature, whether they are internal or external to the corporation.

A mature environmental scanning process will identify many issues whose impact and timing will not qualify them for inclusion in the strategic planning process via issues management. Though some issues will be external to the organization and public in nature, appearing to be beyond the influence of any one organization, some of these issues will still merit appropriate organizational responses. The art of directing and managing these responses is part of issues management. Working with the models and principles described above, issues managers seek to identify potential emerging issues early enough for effective, efficient anticipatory action. This search for tomorrow's issues begins with an effective environmental scanning capability.

Environmental scanning systems have two natural components—one focused on external sources and one focused on internal sources. Today, over thirty years after the pioneering work of Dr. Louis Aguilar, environmental scanning seems like a natural function—every executive is involved at least implicitly in scanning virtually all the time.[2] Accordingly, it may seem unnecessary to formalize environmental scanning in an issues management capability. After all, virtually every executive devotes a significant effort to staying informed on the national, industry, and corporate issues of current or future importance. However, surveys of senior executives engaged in such passive scanning invariably show that they are virtually all scanning the same resources. No systematic review of the scope and completeness of these resources is normally made. Moreover, no review, formal or informal, of recent, current, and expected emerging issues is made to explore what scanning resources need be added to achieve the earliest practical detection of similar issues in the future.

It is not at all uncommon, for example, to find a corporation with recurring issues related to the growing participation of women in the labor force and in ever higher management positions that at the same time has no senior executive regularly scanning resources that have historically caused these issues to surface first. This is why active scanning systems are designed and built with some rigor and formality. If the informal passive scanning systems were working satisfactorily, issues management would not be needed.

To design an external scanning system that builds on, supplements, and supports the existing informal scanning resources, it is best to begin with a review of the informal resources and the results they are producing. This review will identify both the emerging issues as well as the strengths and weaknesses of the existing system—the needs the more formal scanning system will be required to fulfill.

INTERNAL SOURCES

Many of the emerging issues important to an organization are already known to one or more senior executives and other members of the corporation's strategic management and larger corporate family. Too frequently, this becomes evident only in hindsight. Though one executive may know about an emerging issue, he or she often has little or no opportunity to make that knowledge available to other corporate leaders. Thus, the whole of the organization knows substantially less than its parts.

To get a good assessment of the issues already recognized by some senior executives, it is useful to begin with a survey of those senior executives. This will make the whole organization as smart as its parts. This survey usually begins quite informally in small discussions and personal interviews as part of the process of recognizing that an issues management capability is needed. Indeed, it may at first be no more than an expansion of the issues cited as examples of the need for an issues management capability.

The search for issues must be carefully bounded in several different ways. Scanning is not a wholesale search for all possible emerging issues—lest it always produce the same major fears. Another oil embargo, the return of double-digit inflation, recession, nuclear accident, and the like are all possibilities. It is a search for a special kind of emerging issues, those that contain an element of surprise—surprise to the organization in that, as far as is evident to others, the senior executives who will have to deal with a surprise issue are not yet prepared to do so. In other words, these are emerging issues that are not within the strategic vision of the organization's future, not in its interesting future.

A return of double-digit inflation probably no longer qualifies as such a surprise. Senior management, it may be presumed, is well aware of this possibility and has already made appropriate contingency plans such as cost escalators, fuel adjustment clauses, and the like. If a new impact of double-digit inflation were found that is not in the contingency plans, this new impact would be a qualifying surprise.

Issue surveys require the participation of the most senior executives. Who but those familiar with current and planned operations of the corporation can see the potential importance of an emerging issue? The initial survey is usually part of the process of introducing the issues management concept to the senior executives who will be both participants and users of it. This introductory process may occur in small meetings or personal interviews where the purpose and use of issues nominated for the issues management process are made clear.

It is often helpful to have a half-dozen or more sample issues to stimulate the discussion. Several of these might be clearly identified as "wild cards"— issues that will demonstrate the outer bounds of the area being surveyed. The wild cards demonstrate that controversial, unusual, and extreme ideas are meant to be included. Thus, in 1979 a major international bank included the legalization of recreational drugs as one of its issues because tellers who are legally "high" could not be terminated although they are unlikely to count very well. As in this example, for issues that are really wild, it is valuable to outline the possible impact paths that might not be obvious to others.[3]

Since many executives are reluctant to be associated with ideas that are too wild from today's perspective, it is valuable to assure that no inputs will be attributed to any single individual. To guarantee that this path is available, executives are encouraged to nominate new issues anonymously at any time. The importance of anonymity cannot be overemphasized, especially in the first survey for emerging issues. Because the issues management concept is new and not yet defined within the operating experience of most senior executives, no one wants to be associated with what might come to be seen as screwball ideas. If the issues, however wild or poorly stated, do not get nominated, then the issues management system and the corporation cannot address them. Several follow-up invitations for anonymous nominations are used.

Anonymity can be offered at two levels: total anonymity as just outlined or anonymity outside the I/M group. As discussed later, there are circumstances where the author will want to be identifiable to the I/M group to preserve his or her interest or leadership role if an issue action task force is assembled. For more on this idea, see Chapter 9.

A second part of an issues survey focuses on the resources executives use to identify emerging issues. This is not just what current magazines and newspapers the executive scans, but all sources, whatever the medium — TV, radio, newsletters, personal and professional networks, conferences, and the like. When the results of the resources survey are compiled, they invariably show an extremely narrow range of resources: most senior executives scan the same resources. Usually, these include the local paper, major national newspapers and weekly news magazines, complemented by industry and trade publications. For electronic media, most executives scan as time allows local and national evening news, public issues programs, and weekly talk shows.

A cross-check between these sources and the emerging-issues list shows the areas that need more coverage. A sample survey form is shown in Figure 5.1.

Because of the way in which issues evolve and the different needs for corporations to be alerted at different stages, there is no single list of resources to scan. Most issues pass through the literature and media on a well-identified path, spreading from the narrow, highly focused sources to ever broader publications and media with larger and larger audiences. In a sense, an issue spreads through the various publications and other media like a drop of oil on water, as illustrated in Figure 5.2.

Usually, issues are born, or make their debuts, in some highly specialized, limited-circulation publication or within some small group of those most interested and involved. For a pollution issue, a publication like the Sierra Club's *Sierra* might be first. A consumer issue might appear first in *Mother Jones.* A science and technology issue might appear first in AAAS's *Science* or the British Journal *Nature.* Many health care and medical issues often start in *The Journal of the American Medical Association, The New England Journal of Medicine,* or the British journal *Lancet.*

If an issue continues to grow (many don't), it is likely to appear next in a less-specialized source covering a broader spectrum of issues — reaching a larger audience. It may appear in a special weekly section of a major newspaper such as the *New York Times's* special Tuesday section, "Science Times" or the *Washington Post's* health care section. For electronic media, National Public Radio's daily program, *All Things Considered,* usually presents issues ahead of the major television network news programs.

Issues that survive and expand will eventually be recognized by broader publications, perhaps next reaching one of the sections in *Time* or *News-*

Figure 5.1
Internal Issues Survey Form

SAMPLE GENERIC INTERNAL ISSUES SURVEY FORM

What issue do you see that might emerge in the external or internal environment which, if it develops without any response from us, will be important to the current or planned operations, markets, products, suppliers, etc.? Use one form for each emerging issue.

Why is this important? Is it a Threat?___ Opportunity?___ Both?___

What department or functions will be most affected? How?

What sources can be used to track the issue?

What resources and research, if any, are available?

What is the timing of the issue--near term to long term?

Who are other stakeholders?

Is there regulatory recognition of the issue? Media recognition?

What strategies are available?

Who is most likely to be responsible for handling the issue?

---

week or the general news sections of major newspapers. Public television's *MacNeil/Lehrer News Hour* presents a more in-depth look at issues in this stage.

In later stages, network news probably will pick up the issue, or it will appear on the news magazine shows such as ABC's *20/20* or CBS's *60 Minutes*.

Figure 5.2
The Oil Spot Model: The Spread of Issues through Popular Media

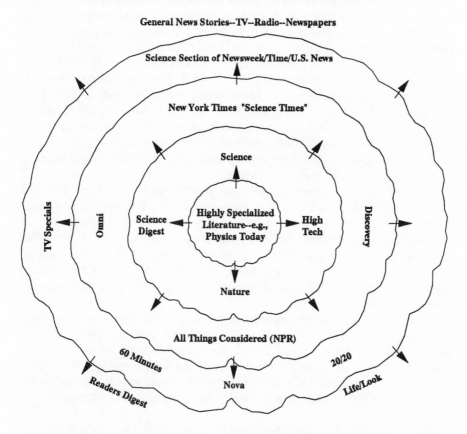

Finally, the issue moves to the broadest circulation in the popular media. For publications, this includes the *Readers Digest*. In the broadcast media, it includes the so-called "info-tainment" market — TV specials, TV movies, and miniseries, as well as films focused on one or more issues. Obviously, at this stage, these are not new issues but issues reaching new audiences. As always with issues, it is important how even mature issues are presented to broad audiences, which are major components of public opinion. Since those who define an issue win the debate, how it is presented to the largest publics is important, even when the issue has already been defined to those more closely involved. General public opinion will be based on these sources, and opinion is still fact.

The path of evolution through the media varies with each issue. Exceptions abound: cold fusion, for example, started out as a "front page story." The pesticide *alar,* commonly used on apples, jumped from obscurity to *60*

Minutes. Such extreme exceptions generate great controversy about how and why the intermediate steps were skipped. Also, they tend to lack the momentum and staying power of issues that have evolved along more traditional paths. A scanning system must be sufficiently robust in its resources to tolerate a wide variation in paths of issues. This means some redundancy needs to be built in.

The kinds of resources scanned then have two dimensions: in addition to deciding what subject areas are to be scanned, the corporation must ask how early it wants and needs to know about emerging issues of each particular type. This mix of what and when is unique for each corporation. Nevertheless, because of the broad reach of some kinds of issues, a few resources are on many scanning resource lists, though not always for the same reasons. Usually, these resources include some of those already covered by many, if not most, senior executives.

In addition, most issues-management professionals have their favorite sources. Some like *Vital Speeches,* since new ideas often appear in speech form even before the established literature or media have the chance to put together a story about them. Major national conferences of issue groups offer a similar leading-edge capability. Other professionals like publications of think tanks and other leading institutions. Education's *The Chronicle of Higher Education* is a favorite. Responsible public-issues programs on television and radio are also popular.

Other key sources for emerging issues are the arts, film, and literature. Here, the focus is not on the highest quality but on what is popular with the public. What message is popular with the public? What kind of books are on the best seller list? What TV shows enjoy the highest ratings? It is a reasonable assignment for every senior executive to read at least one book on the best seller list and see at least one of the current top-rated movies and TV programs.

The literature on scanning has focused on the largest, most formal systems of major corporations and associations. They sound cumbersome, expensive, time consuming, and burdensome—and for the most part they are. Well-meaning advocates of the general concept of scanning talk and dream of incredibly complex systems, with "issue" or "scan" reporting forms feeding into computerized scanning systems. Forgetting the purpose of scanning, some advocates seem more interested in building state-of-the-art data banks; they would have every executive doing as much scanning as those providing commercial scanning services. This is hardly necessary, practical, or desirable. The simpler the system is, the better.

At the outset, there is no reason for a scanning system to be based on paper; it is enough to put new resources on emerging issues into the hands of senior executives on the "rip and read" basis mentioned above. When an issue draws enough attention, executives will start passing around articles and news reports to augment and stimulate their discussions. At this point, usually in the first year, someone concerned about the issue will start to collect articles. The scanning system's issue files will be born, not as a huge bureaucratic monster somewhere in the bowels of the organization but of necessity right in the executive offices.

If a corporation's library already gets a full set of current publications, is not the scanning system duplicative? Some subscriptions certainly will be, but there is a key difference: the scanning subscriptions go to the home addresses of the executives, not their office. The purpose is not to have the publication in the library or at the office, buried in the in-box, but sitting on the nightstand. The purpose is to get its signals of emerging issues into the organization's consciousness.

Another key to keeping a scanning system vibrant is to rotate the assigned resources annually. Usually, participating executives have only one periodical or, at the most, one periodical and one broadcast program to scan at a time. If the size permits, some duplication of key resources is valuable. As the issues management system grows and becomes more structured, the scanning system often becomes more formal. At the outset, though, it is typical for the scanning system to be highly informal, fluid, and unstructured. It is not so much that anyone is assigned to scan a particular resource as it is seeing who has the interest and expertise to best be able to efficiently cover a subject area, by whatever means best suits him or her.

This personal-interest-based scanning needs to be balanced with an organizational-interest-based review. To increase an organization's awareness of an area of concern that has sourced and continued to source important emerging issues, it is useful to give every executive a subscription to the relevant scanning resource(s). It is remarkable how quickly an organizational blindspot will disappear.

Rather than sitting in the in-box at the office, a scanning resource often can get better coverage in a more relaxed setting. Also, as scanning is usually easy reading not requiring prime office time, it can be accomplished in a variety of settings, such as recreation or travel. Since the initial task is to build a sensitivity to emerging issues—an awareness that the signals of change are out there and can be found—the paper documentation and details of more-developed systems can be added later as needed.

When paper is used, the original report, article, or story may be more valuable than even the most insightful executive's summary of it. When the "scan" is brought into the scanning system, other executives will certainly see some additional aspects, interpretations, and implications of an issue. Too much information is lost and too much time is consumed in preparing any formal write-up of an issue. To the scanning process of "rip and read" must be added "pass it on."

Eventually, the scanning files may be centralized in the issues management offices, but even that may be unnecessary for the first year. The key is to put the resources in the hands of those who can see the potential impact of an emerging issue and give these senior executives an opportunity to get their information into the collective knowledge of the corporation. After a survey of internal resources, it will be time to build the external resources.

There is often an overwhelming desire to computerize the scanning system by entering the scanning data into a computer according to some taxonomy. Several extremely large organizations have invested great resources attempting to build computerized systems. The experience of many has been that the benefits of computerization do not yet offset the high costs of having every word and letter pass through a keyboard and having every idea summarized and resummarized. When an organization has the computer technology to enter scanning information by key word and date into a computer file via a simple copier, then the cost-benefits change rapidly and favor computerized scanning systems. Without this technology, experience suggests that computerization is a distraction from the purpose of scanning. Even with advanced input technology, computerization will not be cheap, but the costs of large storage systems are declining rapidly.

External Sources

There are several different approaches to scanning the external environment. Some corporations build a small staff which scans specific resources, though this may be a backup to informal scanning by senior executives. Some rely on the natural instincts of the executives to know what to scan, though as we have seen, their instincts tend to run to the same resources.

Some corporations try to satisfy their needs for intelligence on their environment by buying a scanning service. While many services provide scanning reports, such external services can at best only support internal scanning activities. Who but those fully informed on the current and future operations of the corporation, as well as its changing operating circumstances, can see the potential of an issue to their corporation? Certainly, those outside the agency scanning for many clients cannot. This means that the external scanning system must be operated by the management of the organization. External resources such as various scanning services may be used to supplement the internal scanning system, but they are not a substitute for it. A scanning service is but one input to a scanning system, not the output of one.

Some of the popular *national* scanning resources common to many systems are listed in Appendix A, Figure A.1. These cover only those national issues that are likely to reach most corporations. Industry, technology, and economic, as well as state, local, and regional publications must be included in each individual corporation's system.

These publications are all time-series publications—they continue to come throughout the year. Scanning these is analogous to inserting a filter in a pipeline flowing with information. All executives have a continuous flow of incoming information—of which only some is on paper. Conversations, meetings, conferences, TV, radio are all channels in the information pipeline.

Figure 5.3
Dimensions of Emerging Issues

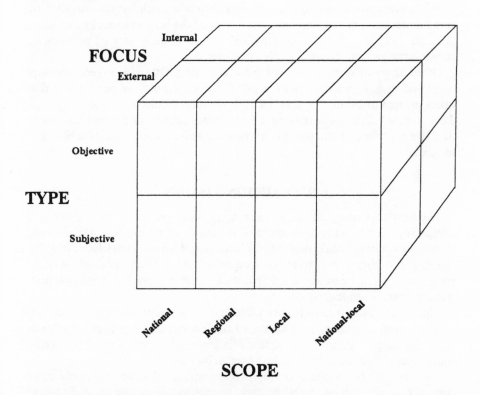

Of course, the filter designed to detect potential emerging issues applies to all of them. In a sense, then, this is a continuous process, a part of all activities, professional and personal.

It is also an open-ended process in that no one knows in advance just what the scanning will produce. Often, the first sense of a new issue will be highly subjective and inferential — some executives will detect or see it and others will not. Just how the human mind recognizes and identifies a whole concept or issue from a few tiny shreds of an idea is far from clear. It is a highly intuitive, right-brain, subjective process. Like perfect pitch, it is a gift some people have while, alas, others are tone deaf. According to current theories that right-brain thinking is sex-linked, women are more likely to succeed in this activity. While no formal research has been done on this, limited empirical evidence suggests this is likely to be true.

As issues develop, their identity becomes less subjective, more objective. At any one time, a scanning system will be discovering and identifying both subjective and objective issues. Along with the two other dimensions of issues already discussed — internal-external and local-national, an "issues space" is defined as shown in Figure 5.3. By examining the spread of issues among the cells in this space, the scanning team can quickly identify any areas that are not being sufficiently covered.

A key element of making the scanning function work for the corporation is the materials that are scanned—the design of the information, to the extent possible, that is flowing in the pipeline. This is an early task of building an issues management capability. See Chapter 6.

Other kinds of scanning must be distinguished. Often, a current development will trigger a memory of a prior article, report, or news story that takes on new meaning. A scan of past resources must be made to find it. This directed scanning is different from either passive or active scanning in that the existence of the piece is known, as well as some idea of where it is located.

RESEARCHING ISSUES

The next two stages of the issues management process—researching and evaluating issues—have an element of the riddle of the chicken and the egg; they are so closely linked that it is difficult to tell which comes first. It is difficult, if not impossible, to make a sophisticated, credible evaluation of an issue until it has been sufficiently defined and explored and its potential impacts have been identified.

This is especially true of highly subjective, embryonic issues whose definition, or even existence, may be based on feelings and hunches. However, since the earliest possible recognition is essential to maximize lead times, these issues must be included, however nebulous.

On the other hand, the scanning process will usually identify many more potential issues than can be adequately researched. Selecting those emerging issues that will be researched, at least well enough for subsequent evaluation, is a key role of the leader of the issues management process. This too is a highly judgmental responsibility, an art and skill that develop from the bond between the unique personality of an individual and his or her perfect match to the needs of the organization.

The Role of Issues Managers

The preliminary researching stage is a process of intelligence gathering, defining, and educating. What is needed at this stage varies according to the nature of the issue. For some issues of first impression, it may be very difficult to identify even a consensus definition of an issue. For other issues, the definition may be clear, but the possible impacts and mechanisms may be too highly speculative.

As in selecting issues for initial research, the issues management leader needs to have a good network both inside and outside the corporation. Although some research materials may exist on a potential emerging issue, when issues are identified at their earliest stages of development (a goal of the scanning system for the most important issues), there may be little or no written materials to research. For this reason, the personal contacts and networks are essential to what often seems like—and is—pioneering issues research.

When an issue is sufficiently well defined, researching, analyzing, and forecasting likely paths of development and their potential impacts are the next step. The difficulty at this stage—foreseeing the potential of issues even before they have much recognition or definition in the society at large—led the pioneers to build networks to exchange ideas and information on resources. Most issues management leaders support their issues research with various informal, open-membership networks. These networks often reach important communities in as many dimensions as possible—vertical, horizontal, geographic, professional, social, political, and so on.

Using all the various research resources and networks, issue managers prepare or oversee the preparation of brief reports, papers, or summaries of the issues—popularly known as "issue briefs." Originally conceived in the early 1970s by the Congressional Research Service for members of Congress, the concept (and in many cases the actual name) has been adopted by issues management programs—from the White House to the American Society of Mechanical Engineers, to United Airlines, to the National Governors' Association, to some electric utilities.

Whatever the name, issue briefs have several aspects in common: first, they define and explain the issue; second, they explore the various positions, sides, and options for the issue and its various interested parties; third, they explore the nature, timing, and mechanisms of the potential impacts of the issue; finally, they provide guidance to additional, more detailed resources, whether in people or paper form. A generalized issue brief might look something like this:

ISSUE BRIEFS: Sample Contents

Introduction: Issue Definition
1. Background and Current Status
2. Forecasts of Potential Importance
   A. Nature of impact
   B. Timing of impact
   C. Precursor events
   D. Monitoring posts
3. Major Stakeholders
   A. Key interests
   B. Goals
   C. Strengths and weaknesses
4. Key Alternatives Futures
   A. Decision points
   B. External forces
   C. Impacts on stakeholders

5. Emerging Agenda
   A. Legislative schedule
   B. Court cases
   C. Other forums
6. Additional Resources
   A. Scanning articles
   B. Literature
   C. Books
   D. External resources and contacts
   E. Internal contact

As issue briefs are designed to be educational tools, and hence have a significant circulation among the senior and upper management, they seldom contain confidential strategies and rarely even explore alternative strategies. As early-warning educational tools about potential issues, they are quite different from formal position papers about current issues, though they may help prepare senior executives for the policy and strategy review process that may eventually lead to a position paper.

Some corporations are reluctant to have any more than the shortest statement of an issue written down, fearing that tomorrow it will be leaked to the press to be spattered across front pages all over the country. Thus, at least initially, issue briefs are treated in some corporations as highly confidential, proprietary reports, as befits intelligence reports on possible threats and opportunities. Other corporations promote the widest possible circulation of their issue briefs, not only within these corporations but to the general public and to any interested party on a request basis — as does Congress.

Clearly, these extremes are not for all corporations — and not for all issues. While most formal issues management groups have some general policy about distribution of issue briefs, materials, reports, and papers, they adjust this to the particular nature of the issue. Obviously, an issues management leader does not want to inadvertently draw attention to or promote the development of an issue by researching and reporting on it.

The distribution policy is not static, but it usually changes as the issues management capability grows. In most corporations, the initial circulation is limited to senior management. Later, the circulation is broadened, though many, but not all, stop short of the general public. Even those with broad circulation policies present their newest issues to their core senior management first, before going on to other audiences.

Issue briefs have to be updated from time to time. Since issues themselves tend to have short lives, issue briefs do also. Some large organizations with substantial resources, such as the Congressional Research Service, update their issue briefs monthly or more frequently, if developments warrant. Most corporations conduct quarterly reviews and annual updates of their issue briefs unless developments require earlier action.

Some issue managers prepare or are deeply involved in preparing the first issue briefs. Later, issue briefs are prepared either by staff or under the direction of the executives who first identified the issue. In some corporations, those who first identify the issue have a "right first refusal" to lead the team that will research and prepare the issue brief. While not overburdening one executive or department, this approach serves to reward to those who first spot an issue by building them into issues management response from the very beginning. At the same time, it discourages executives from withholding issues lest they lose the leadership opportunity. The level of effort involved usually serves as a sufficient deterrent against an executive's or a department's taking on any but its most vital issues.

As this necessarily involves issues research, the issues management team will need the services of a good research librarian from time to time. Even such a librarian will need special issues resources like those listed in Appendix C.

EVALUATING ISSUES: THE ROLE OF SENIOR MANAGEMENT

Since these two stages—environmental scanning and issues research—identify more issues than any corporate management can effectively address, some screening is necessary. This screening is accomplished in a variety of formal and informal techniques.

The least formal means is a judgmental process by the CEO. With or without the results of scanning or issues research, some CEOs make their own personal assessments of emerging issues and their potential significance. As the complexity and number of issues have grown, this has become ever more difficult and time consuming to do well. Most CEOs spread this evaluation process among their senior executives even if they reserve final decisions for themselves.

The involvement of senior management may be as informal as walking a list around by the issues management leader—that is, individual discussions with selected senior executives. It may be a much more formal evaluation process at an annual strategic management meeting. In the formal process, issues might be evaluated for their potential positive and negative impacts, probability, lead time, the ability of the corporation to influence the issue or its impacts and other parameters important to the impact of the issue on the corporation. Senior managers making these evaluations might use one of the recognized group-judgment techniques, such as the nominal group technique (NGT) or the Delphi process.[4]

Care must be taken at this stage that the right questions are asked. An evaluation stage that focuses on potential importance inevitably leads to issues being prioritized by their *net* importance. At best, issues primarily presenting threats are mixed with those primarily presenting opportunities. At worst, the threats and opportunities aspects of individual issues get mixed,

Figure 5.4
Evaluation of Emerging Issues

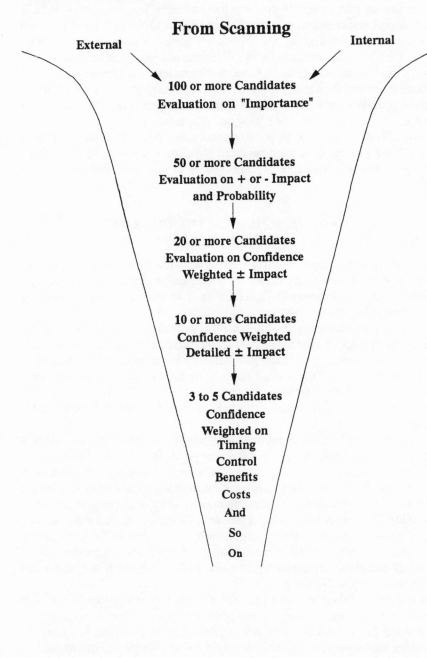

From Scanning

External   Internal

100 or more Candidates
Evaluation on "Importance"

50 or more Candidates
Evaluation on + or - Impact
and Probability

20 or more Candidates
Evaluation on Confidence
Weighted ± Impact

10 or more Candidates
Confidence Weighted
Detailed ± Impact

3 to 5 Candidates
Confidence
Weighted on
Timing
Control
Benefits
Costs
And
So
On

and the evaluations have no useful meaning. Moreover, the opportunity will be lost to develop both strategies that enhance desirable impacts and different strategies that mitigate or avoid undesirable impacts. Obviously, such a process is of limited value. At a minimum, both the threat and the opportunity aspects of each issue must be evaluated separately.

This still has major problems. The top issues may include those over which the organization has little influence or no practical, cost-effective role. A second evaluation must be made to determine the relative influence of the organization. The high highs — high in either threat or opportunity *and* high in cost-effective influence by the organization — become the focus of the strategy stage. Issues falling in the other three groups — high lows, low highs, and low lows — are tracked by the issues management staff for their potential movement to other categories.

A flow of the evaluation process is shown in Figure 5.4. To find the three to five key issues that will become the focus of issue action programs, issue managers often start with one hundred or more and a rough "importance" evaluation. In each stage, the number of issues decreases and the evaluation detail increases. This keeps the total number of evaluations in each round roughly constant. With modern decision-support software such as vote weighting and tallying programs, these evaluations can be accomplished very rapidly.[5] It is not unusual for a group of executives to accomplish the entire process of identifying, refining, and evaluating more than 100 issues in a six-to-eight-hour evaluation session.

At the early stages, the results of many issues are evaluated in terms of a simple two-dimensional matrix, such as impact vs. probability, as shown in Figure 5.5.

It is important not only where a single issue lands but where a family of similar issues lands. For example, what kind of issues — social, technical, legislative — have high positive impact but low probability? Is there a balance, or are like issues grouped together? What do the groupings say about the evaluation process? Executives love technological change, for example, but fear social change. What do the groupings say about the scanning system?

One health care organization, for example, found that 80 percent of its top issues were driven by technology — only to realize not only that there was no vice-president for technology in the senior management but also that the group confidence for technology issues was the lowest. Before any response to emerging technologies was undertaken, the senior management had to "get smart" enough about emerging medical technologies to evaluate them confidently.

In a major Department of Defense study for the army chief of staff, a panel of army generals suggested that all major issues facing military leadership for the next forty years derive from the application of computer technologies. While this was seen as descriptive of many issues of the past forty

Figure 5.5
Impact–Probability Chart

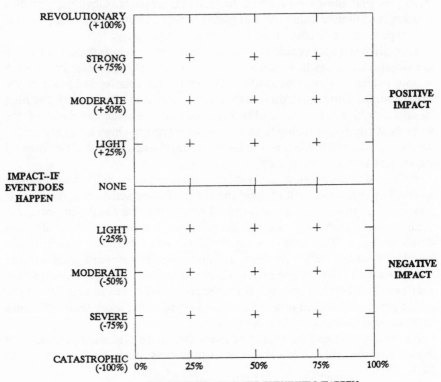

PROBABILITY THAT THE EVENT WILL HAPPEN

years, it was fundamentally an extrapolative view of the future. After some discussion of these preliminary issues, the generals repeated the evaluation process and produced more credible results.[6]

The probability-impact matrix is only one of many possible useful matrixes. Others include impact vs. ability to influence, cost vs. benefit, lead time vs. response time, risk vs. reversibility.

As an issue management process matures, additional important screenings can be added. The probability, timing, availability, and reliability of precursor events, adequacy of lead time, and the like can be added. In these advanced stages, additional analyses of group opinion are used to clarify the issues evaluation process. This allows for confidence weighting, measurements of consensus, and prompt, clear feedback of group opinions. In confidence weighting, executives weight their contribution to the group opinion by the confidence they have in their own expertise. Rather than "one person, one vote," the opinion of the group is weighted toward those

Figure 5.6
Renfro's Cube

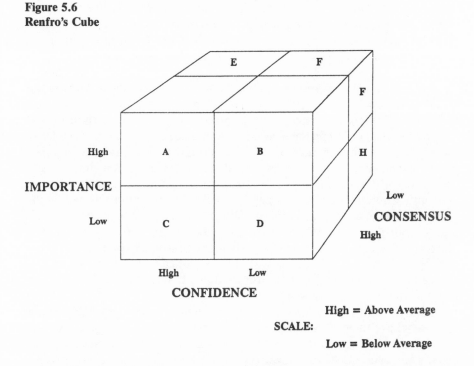

IMPORTANCE

High   A   B   H

Low   C   D

High   Low
CONFIDENCE

Low
CONSENSUS
High

High = Above Average

SCALE:

Low = Below Average

who have, or believe they have, more expertise on the issue. This prevents the opinion of an expert from being offset by someone else's guess.

Results of the confidence-weighted evaluation process are analyzed in terms of three factors—group opinion, group average confidence, and group consensus. This analysis can be summarized by locating the cells according to the factors listed above in Renfro's cube, as shown in Figure 5.6.

If consensus is low for a particular issue, then the executives need to review alternative assumptions, to review and refine the issue definition before repeating its evaluation. If confidence is low, they need to be better educated about the issue; a special presentation might be scheduled for the next meeting of the issues evaluation group.

The first key question to ask when the evaluations are complete is, "Do the results really reflect our future as we see it?" This is not a trivial question. Neither does it mean to challenge the evaluation process. Rather, it is a test of credibility. It is not uncommon to see the future through the past—to believe that the greatest changes in the future will be like those that have generated the most trouble recently. That may well be so, but it is likely that the future will be richer than the past, offering up new kinds of challenges that have not been prominent. If the top rankings are dominated by one or two kinds of issues (legislative, regulatory, or technological, for example), then the scanning, issues research, and evaluation process need to be examined for balance and completeness. If more than half of the most important issues are of a single kind, chances are this is the case.

The relative position of the issues in each of the rankings has several different meanings. For example, how do the top issues of a given category fall in other rankings — what is the confidence and consensus of the group on these issues? What is the ability of the corporation to influence these issues? Is it cost effective? While the position of each issue has meaning, the relative positions of entire categories also are important. Low confidence in a particular category of issues may indicate the need for the group either to add executives with that expertise or to increase its own expertise.

Another question asks which parts of the corporation are affected by the various positive and negative issues? While it is common to focus on developing strategies in response to particular issues, it may also be important to develop strategies focused on the particular departments and sections that will be anticipating and dealing with the most change. So many issues may have impact on human resources, for example, that strategies for increasing the capabilities of this department may be indicated.

Finally, for the top three to five remaining issues, it is not enough to know that they have the highest threat and opportunity, coupled with the highest risk-benefit; it is essential to know just which departments, missions, products, and functions of the organization will be impacted. This calls for a microevaluation. Because this is so detailed, it is practical only for the final set of issues.

The first step in making a microevaluation of an issue is to determine the dimension of the organization to be examined. Nearly always, this first dimension is the departmental one — human resources, finance, production, R&D, transportation, materials, or government relations. The second step is to evaluate the relative weights of these subdivisions, using the same scale as that used for evaluating the events. The final step is the actual evaluation of each issue on each of the departments just as was done for the entire corporation. The department-weighted totals for each issue are calculated at the right edge. The results will look like the sample shown in Figure 5.7.

It is not unusual for these microresults to disagree with the earlier corporatewide macroevaluations. However, it is always illuminating why the macro and microresults differ.

The results of this microevaluation are more than just detailed information about how and where already-identified emerging issues impact the corporation. This detailed information supports the development of strategies that are focused on each individual vertical dimension — in this case, each individual department.

This analysis is focused on a single department across all issues. The leaders of these departments (e.g., the vice president of human resources), as well

Figure 5.7
Detailed Importance Evaluation

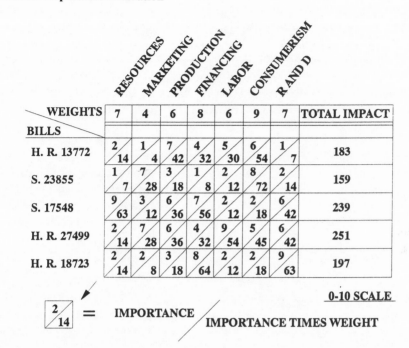

	RESOURCES	MARKETING	PRODUCTION	FINANCING	LABOR	CONSUMERISM	R AND D	TOTAL IMPACT
WEIGHTS	7	4	6	8	6	9	7	
BILLS								
H. R. 13772	2/14	1/4	7/42	4/32	5/30	6/54	1/7	183
S. 23855	1/7	7/28	3/18	1/8	2/12	8/72	2/14	159
S. 17548	9/63	3/12	6/36	7/56	2/12	2/18	6/42	239
H. R. 27499	2/14	7/28	6/36	4/32	9/54	5/45	6/42	251
H. R. 18723	2/14	2/8	3/18	8/64	2/12	2/18	9/63	197

0-10 SCALE

2/14 = IMPORTANCE

IMPORTANCE TIMES WEIGHT

as other senior executives, now have the opportunity to develop strategies for the department across all emerging issues. The CEO and senior leadership now have new information about the threats and opportunities facing the various departments. Strategies based on individual departments can now be identified and implemented. This information also provides guidance in the allocation of resources and priorities among departments.

This process is repeated for several independent dimensions of the organization. After the departmental dimension, a dimension based on the missions of the organization is usually analyzed, followed by functions or products or stakeholders. The results of a series of these complex evaluations is a very detailed picture of the interaction of the organization with key issues in its emerging external environment.

The final issues—those having the best combination of impact, influence, and cost-benefit—move to the next stage, strategy development. There are seldom more than a half-dozen of these at any one time, usually only two or three. Issues near, but not at, the top are kept under close, continuing tracking and monitoring for any changes that could move them into the top ranks. While the leader of the issues management group plays a major role in organizing, analyzing, and presenting issues to the evaluation group, he or she does not have the authority to either make or implement strategies designed to anticipate issues.

Just as the comptroller keeps the books on the corporation's assets but does not have any independent authority to spend them, the issues management group keeps the books on emerging issues but does not have any standing or independent authority to address them. For the continued successful operation of an issues management capability, it is essential that all interested parts and parties in the corporation be aware of this. No executives need fear that the issues management group will get involved in their issues without their knowledge.

Based on the results of the evaluation stage, the CEO and senior management determine the response of the corporation to each issue. This may vary from instructing the issues management group to conducting additional in-depth research to identifying options, developing alternative strategies, or forming an issue team or task force. For those issues where a response is needed, the CEO usually delegates the task to an issues operations team.

DEVELOPING ISSUE STRATEGIES:
THE ROLE OF ISSUE TEAMS

The CEO and senior management can use any of the resources of the corporation to respond to an emerging issue. It is not at all unusual for a variety of skills to be needed to develop and implement the corporate strategy in response to a major emerging issue — from government relations, to public affairs, to community relations, human resources, or advertising. The issues management group is but one of the resources that may be called upon. In practice, the issues management group usually plays a major supportive role in issue action teams. Issue teams are frequently led either by a senior executive or by the senior executive responsible for the area most affected by the issue.

The interdisciplinary nature of issue teams borrows heavily from the matrix management concept. The first task of issue teams is frequently to develop a much more complete picture of the issue, its future, and the potential opportunities and risks presented to the corporation. This is a research task for which the issues management group is well suited and in which it often plays a major role. Based on this additional research, the issue team develops strategies and action plans for review and selection by the CEO. As the issue team moves more into issue action plans, the research role often decreases and the issues management group provides other staff support to the team.

IMPLEMENTING ISSUE STRATEGIES

The selection and implementation of strategies are the responsibilities of senior management. To avoid any possible misunderstanding of the role and purpose of the issues management group, it usually has no independent authority to act on issues. In this sense, as noted earlier, issues management is an intelligence function that does not get involved in the "operations side" unless specifically directed to do so. Such strict adherence to this distinction reduces the chance that the issues management group will be seen by any other part of the corporation as meddling in its issues. By involving the issue teams representatives from departments that have an interest in the issue, the chance for conflict and confusion are reduced. For the same reason, leadership of the issue team is usually placed in the hands of a "line" executive or one who has substantive responsibility at stake rather than in the hands of a "staff" person from the issues management group.

The one exception to these general operating principles is the CEO who heads his or her own issues management team. Obviously, such a CEO has independent authority. The more senior the leader of the issues management function is, the closer he or she is to having independent authority. For issues management leaders who are below the senior management level—that is, who are not members of the executive committee—the distinction between the appropriate intelligence gathering and inappropriate operations becomes necessary.

OVERSIGHT OF ISSUES MANAGEMENT AND STRATEGIES

Like all management functions, issues management needs periodic oversight and review. Since issues management is not closely connected to immediate operations and the bottom line, it is difficult to determine the effectiveness and value of an issues management capability. Since the goal of issues management is to anticipate emerging issues well in advance, it necessarily is several years after an issues management system begins to operate before it has a track record to be evaluated. Hence, oversight depends on the maturity of the issues management system.

For systems that are being built, oversight focuses on the goals and schedules that have been set. Is the capability being developed? Are the goals being met? Do they need to be modified? Because these evaluations are pretty objective and straightforward, they can be readily accomplished.

Evaluations of mature operating systems are more difficult. Since a goal is to identify emerging issues, issues management can be evaluated on whether the identification of issues is early enough. But what about the issues that have not yet been identified at all? It is difficult to tell today that the system has missed an important issue. Some time later it may become painfully obvious, but today it is not clear.

Evaluations of the issues research and evaluation stages follow traditional oversight lines. Is the quality there? Is it timely? Are the most important issues getting to the top? Is it cost effective?

Ultimately, the oversight of an entire issues management system requires a qualitative, subjective judgment of its key customers—the senior manage-

Figure 5.8
Issues Management Process

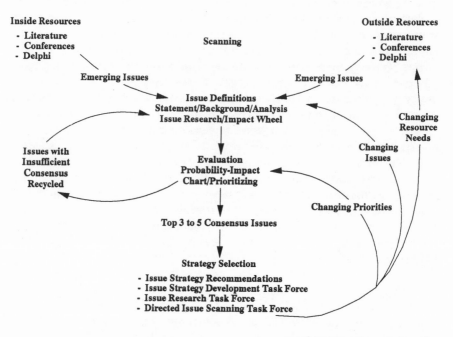

ment. If the issues management system is working well, senior management will, at a minimum, feel more confident in making decisions about the future. The corporation will have more of a sense of direction, control, and purpose. There will be fewer upsets, crises, and unpleasant surprises, though it is not always clear just how much of this can be attributed to successful issues management and how much to other factors. More than 2600 years ago, the Chinese philosopher Lao-tzu observed that a leader leads best when, after the goal is achieved the followers say, "We did it ourselves!" This axiom often seems to apply to successful issues management.

THE ISSUES MANAGEMENT CYCLE

When an issues management system matures, it will begin to develop a natural cycle of issues identification, research, evaluation, and strategy preparation. The pace of the cycle depends on several factors. Many organizations time the cycle to their annual planning cycle, building an issues component into their strategic plan. Others time their cycle to the natural process of their major legislative and regulatory issues at the state or federal level. An annual cycle with flexibility for rapidly moving issues, legislative schedules, and the like is common.

Part of this cycle includes reviewing the distribution and content of the scanning system. Also, updating or archiving existing issue briefs, reports, and files, as well as research methods and resources, is undertaken. Finally, the evaluation criteria and the results they produce are reviewed and updated. Some organizations rotate their executives through a year or two of high involvement with the issues process to assure that future leaders will be well prepared to deal with their rapidly changing environment. The continuous adjusting and refining cycle of the key stages of issues management is summarized in Figure 5.8.

The calendar for an annual issues management cycle includes both continuous and discrete tasks. Environmental scanning runs continuously throughout the year; periodically, the results of the scanning process are reviewed with some minimum formality. Issues research also continues throughout the year. The research results are used to prepare issue briefs and consulted in the periodic evaluations and reevaluations of the issues.

The formal evaluation and reevaluation of emerging issues by senior management is conducted once a year, usually in conjunction with the annual strategic planning session. With fresh results in hand, the senior management can authorize any issue operations that are needed. The annual issues management cycle is shown in Figure 5.9 (on p. 92).

Figure 5.9
Annual Issues Management Calendar

Scanning: Continuous

   Annual emerging issues survey

   Annual review of scanning assignments

First Quarterly Scanning Review

       * Selection of issues for research

       * Refinement of scanning resources

       * Update scanning categories

       * Review/oversight of issue operations

       and plans, if any

Hot issues
Needing
Immediate Action

Second Quarterly Scanning Review

       Preliminary evaluation of issues

       Repeat quarterly reviews (*) listed above

Third Quarterly Scanning Review

       First re-evaluation of issues

       Preliminary list of issues

       Repeat quarterly reviews (*) listed above

Fourth Quarterly Scanning Review

       Final re-evaluation of issues

       Final list of issues

   Repeat quarterly reviews (*) above

Present to
Senior
Management

Annual review and oversight of IM Program

   Repeat cycle

6

Purposes and Missions

The overriding objective of an issues management system is to enhance the current and long-term performance and standing of the corporation by anticipating change, promoting opportunities, and avoiding or mitigating threats. Attaining this objective, of course, promotes the performance and standing of the corporate leadership, both within and outside the corporation, but this is secondary for issues management systems in publicly-held corporations.

Just as issues management capabilities come in a variety of forms, they also serve this overriding objective through a variety of purposes and missions. While the four basic stages — scanning and issue detection, issue research and analysis, prioritizing, and strategy development — are present in all issues management systems, however formal or informal, their form is determined first and foremost by their purpose and mission.

Currently, issues management systems in the United States — whether in private, public, or not-for-profit organizations — serve one or more of six key missions.[1] For most organizations, these missions are hierarchical — the higher-level missions include the lower ones. The strategies and resources used to implement them vary according to the mission focus as shown in Figure 6.1.

FOCUS 1: SENIOR MANAGEMENT

Issues management plays a key role at the highest level of corporate strategy development. It is a necessary component of product planning, market strategy, and corporate strategic planning. Because of the proprietary nature of corporate strategies and even of the process of strategy development, this

Figure 6.1
Purposes and Missions of an Issues Management Function

Focus 1:

Senior Management
Role: Strategic Management

Focus 2:

Internal Corporate Members

Role: Communicate Strategic Issues/Plans

Focus 3:

The Extended Corporate Family

Role: Early warning, Participation, Continuity/Direction

Focus 4:

The Industry and Its Environment

Role: Anticipate & Respond to Strategic Industry-Wide Issues

Focus 5:

Investors, Opinion Leaders, Other Unique Publics

Role: Corporate Positioning on Strategic Issues

Focus 6:

The General Public

Role: Provide Drive and Direction to I/M at Other Levels

focus of issues management virtually becomes a trade secret. Only the most general, vague terms are used in describing the issues management systems at this level — much less the resources, personnel, or services used by it. Even the outside designers of such systems are allowed only glimpses of their operation or substantive output at this level in private corporations. For the system to retain its options and preserve its effectiveness, specific issues action strategies must remain highly confidential, particularly as they are linked to particular business strategies. While one might infer possible strategies behind issue actions, it is essential from the corporate view that they remain just that, inferences. Shell Oil Company's strategy for responding to the TransAfrica boycott over its South African operations was effectively wiped out when the key strategy document was leaked to the press. The focus of issue action strategies at this level is highly specific and proprietary, as well as time and resource critical.

FOCUS 2: INTERNAL CORPORATE MEMBERS

Here, leadership on emerging issues is focused internally on the corporation and its corporate family—its management, staff, and employees. In a sense, although this focus is still proprietary, it is but public within the corporation. In this area, the issues management system improves the performance of the organization in an implicit role rather than an explicit one. The issues management system provides a forum for input throughout the organization into the policy and strategy development process. This addresses several key organizational issues. First, it provides access and a sense of participation down through the organization structure. Second, it provides a sense of continuity and stability as new policy directions and necessary administrative changes occur, improving corporate flexibility and response time.

Perhaps the greatest value of an internal focus is its potential to provide the vital sense of direction and purpose for the organization and its employees. Thus, in the early 1980s when the World Bank seemed to lurch from crisis to crisis and many executives sensed a lack of foresight, vision, and direction—a sense of being adrift in a sea of change—the issues management system was made more formal and prominent. Even if it never formally "managed" the World Bank's resources in anticipating a single external issue, it did manage this internal one.

Corporations with issues management systems focused at this level find it more effective if they do not publicize their work. At a professional meeting in the late 1980s, Dr. Walter Albers of General Motors described part of GM's internal system—as it was organized and operated ten years earlier. He declined to describe any more recent developments, though it was certainly clear that this "old" pioneering work was continuing into the present.[2]

FOCUS 3: THE EXTENDED CORPORATE FAMILY

A corporation does not stand alone but in an environment composed of its customers, clients, and suppliers. Where emerging issues are forcing change in the immediate environment, it is essential that the corporation include input from its customers, clients, and suppliers in both its scanning and its issue detection system, as well as communicate its issue concerns and research to them. At a minimum, this takes the form of an "issues newsletter." Many organizations use their issues newsletters to not only communicate their issues and concerns but also to provide a scanning resource as sub-scriptions are traded throughout the community of other issues managers. With names like *What's Next?, Corporate Public Issues, FutureSurvey, Straws in the Wind, Tomorrow's Trends, FutureScan, Issue Network, Scan, Over the Horizon,* and *From the Crow's Nest,* these documents have per-mitted a vibrant exchange of new ideas to develop among issues managers. For anyone who is interested but does not have a subscription to exchange, many organizations sell subscriptions to offset production costs.

Security Pacific National Bank, for instance, published an internal news-letter focused on emerging trends and issues. Over a ten-year period, *Future-Scan* evolved from an internal intelligence bulletin to a vehicle to reach the banking community with the message that Security Pacific is a dynamic modern organization in touch with its environment and preparing for its tomorrows. Security Pacific's strategy coincided with the great transition to a deregulated, or at least less regulated and more competitive, banking envi-ronment. Once the regulatory and competitive environment stabilized, Security Pacific spun the newsletter off for private publication.

FutureScan lives on as one of the major private scan newsletters. Another major private newsletter focused more on emerging issues and issues man-agement is *Corporate Public Issues and Their Management,* published by Issue Action Publications. These newsletters, along with *FutureSurvey* from the World Future Society and association newsletters like that of the Issues Management Association are the basic issues management scanning and networking publications vital to building an issues management function.[3]

AT&T's chairman, Charles Brown, and his issues managers, Jim Armstrong and Brook Tunstall, used similar signals during the deregulation of the tele-communications industry to say that old Ma Bell was in reality a thoroughly modern corporation, more than able to meet the challenges of new technol-ogies, new competitors, and a new and unregulated competitive environment.[4] As part of this issues management program, AT&T prepared and published the first public legislative forecasting report, *The Context of Legislation* (based on Renfro's LEGISCAN model) and distributed twenty thousand copies to opinion leaders in the United States and abroad through local operating telephone companies, including copies to all members of Con-gress and of the Canadian Parliament—the legislators working on AT&T's deregulation.[5]

Brown's primary focus was the Washington policy makers themselves whom he addressed directly, though he was careful to address their constit-uents as well through Bell's local subsidiaries. History shows his veracity.

FOCUS 4: THE INDUSTRY AND ITS ENVIRONMENT

While the focus on the immediate environment includes some elements of this industry focus, by being more limited in focus, it is more defensive, more reactive, more a preservation of current and existing business interests and profit centers.

The industry focus is more proactive and future-oriented. The forums most commonly used are those offered by trade and professional associations, industry groups, and more general private sector associations addressing public issues — The Business Roundtable, The Public Affairs Council, The Business-Higher Education Forum. In these forums, the issues management objective is much more explicitly focused by specific strategies and the issues management system's existence is of little importance. The issue research, issue strategy, and issue leader (the CEO of corporate spokesman) — the message and messenger — dominate. Clearly, issues that have just been identified and have yet to reach the formative stages or develop any constituencies seldom if ever appear here.

An organized and somewhat formal system is usually presumed — though this may not be the case. When he was CEO of Textron, William Miller gathered all his input from sources of varying formality and retreated to a quiet place to set priorities, select issues, and establish strategies. He continued this process even as he addressed larger audiences and eventually the general public when he was secretary of the treasury. However, such a personal, private style began to reduce his internal leadership effectiveness — the original focus — but only as he was leaving. Such a private style, while effective in the short term, erodes rather than builds the leadership base. Its applications are primarily limited to exit strategies of the CEO.

Allstate Insurance, the insurance division of Sears Roebuck, has operated at the industry focus level with its series of national conferences on AIDS. From a centralized issues management system under a "Director of Issues Management," Chairman Dick Hayen projected Allstate as an industry leader on this key issue. Allstate did not present any particular solution to the AIDS crisis, but positioned itself either to be a major player in emerging public policy responses to the issues or to be in a key position to anticipate them and their impact.

While keeping a low personal profile, Chairman Hayen established his and Allstate's authority and standing to lead on AIDS issues as he moves Allstate's role to larger publics. When the second session of the 100th Congress convened, Allstate held another major conference on AIDS in Washington, reaching the nation's political and opinion leaders. John Akers, chairman of IBM, has voiced his concern about the AIDS issue in several forums, but he has not involved his corporation in such a public manner.

In a similar vein, The Gannett Corporation — one of America's largest publishers and media corporations, owning the newspaper *USA Today,* as well as many local TV stations and newspapers — sponsors two private conferences (held at plush resorts) each year. At these events, judges and other high government officials hear prominent academics, lawyers, and opinion leaders present Gannett's agenda — from protection of the right of free speech to the contributions of the media to a free society. Gannett's strategy seems to be one of responding to the growing criticism of the press and other media and the continuing decline of public esteem for and confidence in them by anticipating hostile or restrictive legislation, regulations, and court decisions—or of reversing them on higher appeal. Even if its strategy is exposed or judicial ethics were to strengthen, Gannett—unlike other corporations—faces little risk in this quite questionable judicial lobbying: What media would criticize such tactics used to promote their own interests.

FOCUS 5: INVESTORS, OPINION LEADERS, OTHER UNIQUE PUBLICS

Issues management systems focused on investors, opinion leaders, and government regulators have a broad purpose—generating the good will, contacts, public acceptance, trust, and public positioning to be used as needed in specific issues action strategies at this or other levels. The general focus builds reserves in these areas. Such reserves may be established in anticipation of particular needs such as the Gannett case. Weyerhaeuser, for example, sponsors many public issues forums and television public issues programming, always carefully noting that Weyerhaeuser is "the tree growing company." It is almost difficult to imagine, after years of such positioning, that Weyerhaeuser ever cuts down a tree, much less "clear cuts" forests on public lands—but it does. Weyerhaeuser used some of its reserves when it cleared trees felled by Mt. St. Helens volcano—but stirred little issue as it presented this as a conservation effort.

Enlightened corporations now compete for the opportunity to follow the Weyerhaeuser example, especially the many U.S. corporations that drew so little public notice that their stocks fell substantially below book value. IBM, for example, traded in the late 1980s at approximately a quarter of its book value. The importance of such programs assumes a highly personal value to senior executives whose compensation depends in part on stock options.

An example of a broad, proactive focus at this level is the campaign led by Reginald Jones while chairman of General Electric in the early 1980s. GE's issues management system concluded that the public perception of risk had great impact on GE's operations, from nuclear steam supply systems to consumer products. Jones used every public forum available to ask the question, "Can we have a risk-free society?" He drove this home with practical examples—for example, GE could make a hair dryer that would safely withstand immersion in hot water without electrocuting its user . . . for $1200. A dryer that required the good sense to unplug it before reaching into the water to retrieve it costs only $12. He backed his position with statistics on relative risks and, when necessary, the aggressive recall of products of questioned safety. The clear relevance to virtually all GE products and services provided the context and standing for Jones's position. The program provided dividends at all other levels. Though the tort liability issue emerged anyway, Jones kept GE out of the target zone. GM and Ford should have done as well.

Under Jack Welch, GE is overplaying its hand. Its self-portrait of corporate social responsibility has reached overkill and threatens the entire corporate image process. GE hopes the public will forget the unrefuted charge that its use of discarded military engine parts caused the DC-10 crash in Iowa that killed more than eighty people. GE hopes the public will not notice that it has not stopped using discarded parts. And GE hopes the American public will never learn that it bought the Tungstrum Lighting Corporation in Hungary, not to promote international good will and freedom as its ads say but to kill its competition. GE hopes the American public will never learn it destroyed Tungstrum and fired most of its employees. It was this behavior that earned Welch the nickname "Neutron John." Like the neutron bomb, he eliminates the people but leaves the offices and factories standing. GE hopes that the American public will never learn that it has polluted the upper Hudson River so badly with asbestos, dioxins, and other poisons that New York state and the EPA are afraid any cleanup they order will spread the pollution throughout the Hudson. GE hopes this scare will save it the estimated $20 billion in cleanup costs. GE's heavy-handed corporate positioning campaign is reviving the sleaze issue that plagued GE senior management for decades before Regi Jones did his own cleaning.

W. H. Krome George, chairman of ALCOA, found opportunity in waste aluminium cans. An outgrowth of the ecology and environmental protection movement, recycling was an idea whose time had come. The soft-drink industry was—and still is—firmly against mandatory recycling.

Since they were providing an immediate benefit for the consumer, the soft-drink manufacturers were not a suitable target for the environmentalists. The public black eye was being reserved for the can and bottle makers. The bottle makers were decentralized, but as an ultimate source, ALCOA's name was on every waste can—whether ALCOA made it or not. By leading the campaign for recycling, ALCOA could move from a pollution source to an environmental leader. Of course, it helped in the case of aluminium that the economics worked to greatly offset the costs. However, by moving quickly and early, ALCOA seized the initiative and enjoyed broad public acceptance for years.

FOCUS 6: THE GENERAL PUBLIC

A focus on the general public is the most difficult to sustain for a variety of reasons. The first is cost; it is extremely expensive to reach the general public. The second is relevancy; the general public does not expect corporations to bypass the appropriate intermediary institutions and forums in order to address it. Any issue of such national importance does not occur so suddenly as to justify bypassing opportunities to speak to selected segments of the general public first.

In the United States today, an issues management focus on the general public level is so rare as to be an anomaly. Only producers of major national consumer products focus on this level, and then as a secondary theme, add-on, or adjunct to product advertising. General Motors called itself the "corporation of the 21st century," but the signal was so subtle and weak that its claim is noticed only by those who were aware of it because they were members of targeted publics at earlier levels. Chairman Roger Smith conducted carefully planned TV interviews in conjunction with GM's 1989 "Corporation of the Future" exposition, but the exposition was for specific GM publics, by invitation only. When he was pulling Chrysler back from the edge of bankruptcy, Lee Iacocca appeared in Chrysler's advertisements with the slogan: "We just want to be the best." While he said this to the general public, he said it *for* internal Chrysler consumption. And by one measure, Chrysler became the best. By going to the general public, Iacocca resolved an internal issue: Yes, he meant to carry through on his plans for reform.

This in not to say that corporations do not reach the general public. They do and must. But they do so through special messages designed for particular segments or specific parts of the general public.

The various missions of an issues management capability are shown in Figure 6.1. The general direction of growth and development is from the top down. For more discussion on this point, see Chapter 7.

PART III

Organizational Design

7

Building an Issues Management Function: The First Steps

The challenges involved in building an issues management capability into a mature corporation are quite distinct from those involved in running an existing capability. While much has been written on the various styles of issues management systems and stages, with core concepts being generally accepted, little has yet been written on what is emerging as the central question: How does a corporation build an issues management capability?

It is important to recognize that there is no one single design that only has to be applied to the corporation. While the four core stages of issues management are present in all issues management systems, their form and use are particular to the style and personality of each organization. The unique design for a given corporation must be developed under the direction of those most familiar with the existing organization. Usually, successful issues management systems are built to run on the strategic management cycle, often an annual process. Experience has shown it takes at least one complete cycle to build and assemble all components of an issues management capability. Another cycle or two must pass before the system achieves optimal operating effectiveness.

While there is no fixed design, approach, or path to follow, it is possible to identify the key stages, design parameters, and guiding principles that determine both the final design and the approach to building it into a particular corporation. Organizational issues, human resource requirements, and schedule considerations are all important factors. Hence, these classical observations have great meaning:

There is nothing more difficult to carry out, nor more doubtful of success, nor more dangerous to handle, than to initiate a new order of things. For the reformer has enemies in all who profit by the old order, and lukewarm defenders in all those who would profit by the new order. [1]

No new system in an organization can succeed. Only a system grown onto an existing system has any chance of success. [2]

The truth of both these axioms has made building an issues management capability so very difficult and such an important art. While the literature on how issues management and other foresight systems work is slowly being established, the art of building such systems has not yet been addressed. The analogy is to the suspension bridge: once you finally understand the delicate balance that is the key to the design, you are left wondering how in the world the thing could ever be built. The wisdom of these axioms are the core design principles of the building of all successful issues management systems.

IDENTIFYING THE NEED

Building an issues management function involves several key decisions at the beginning and, later on, the careful orchestration of two simultaneous processes. The key decisions at the beginning may be highly visible and explicit or they may be almost invisible and implicit. Whatever the form, it is essential to recognize their existence and to complete them all.

First, there is the recognition by someone in senior management of the need for more and better information or intelligence about the environment of the organization. Simply put, some senior executive recognizes that the organization needs to be changed. In the parlance of organizational development, this is called an intervention. [3]

Notwithstanding how carefully this belief is communicated, some part of the organization will see this as criticism of its performance and a potential threat to its future. Even though an issues management function has not been previously defined and no division or section of the corporation has been assigned the responsibility, it is not difficult to understand that several different divisions or sections might well believe it is their responsibility to accomplish the issues management function or major parts of it — or at least to identify the need for a greater issues management capability.

From an organizational development and change perspective, the earliest presentation of the idea for change must be handled with extreme tact and skill. It is essential that those most directly affected by any change be included in the discussions from the earliest. [4]

Implicit in this early recognition of the need for faster, clearer, earlier intelligence on emerging issues is the recognition of some present capability, however minimal, unarticulated, disjointed, confused, and tardy it may be, for getting information about the changing environment into the organization. It is this capability or noncapability that needs to be analyzed, understood, and incorporated into the development of the more formal issues management function.

More often than not, the drive for better issues intelligence comes not from issues that have a traditional home in the organization (the various departments are probably on top of current issues that affect them) but from issues that emerge with no clear organizational home. These issues appeared between the boxes of the organizational chart and were not addressed early enough. This is a normal phenomenon. The organization's departmental structure was designed in the past to address the needs of the times. Twenty years ago, few corporations had consumer affairs departments or computer services. Today, many do. Issues management is an organizational response to move the identification and anticipation of issues from an ad hoc, fragmented process into the realm of an ongoing function of modern, professional management.

Second, someone must understand the stages and capabilities of an issues management function and have a vision of what advantages it will bring to the organization. The benefits of the proposed change must be presented to and accepted by the key leaders as clearly outweighing the costs of changing the existing system.

Third, someone must define the mission and goals of the issues management function in terms that will be recognized and supported by the strategic management. This involves developing a concept or design of the issues management function that fits within the corporation, both in terms of existing organizational structure and in terms of flow and cycle of the strategic management processes. It also includes some outline of the stages and schedules necessary to build the function, as well as an assessment of necessary resources. These points are covered later.

Finally, someone must be willing to work for acceptance of the issues management concept by the organization, seek authorization to proceed, and guide the issues management function through its early stages of development. This begins with developing an understanding of issues management, its models, processes, stages, capabilities, and, most important, its limitations. Issues management will not put an end to all unpleasant surprises, nor will it identify every issue at its birth. As with people, the sheer number of issues says many of them are being born constantly, but these births rarely happen in public.

DEVELOPING CONCEPTS AND GOALS

Depending on the nature of the organization and the state of the need, the key concepts and goals steps can be developed quickly and informally in a few conversations between the CEO and the issues management champion or advocate. In other organizations it may take years of discussion, debate, and review. While the literature on the issues management process and concepts, as well as studies of similar functions in similar organizations, can be used to help define the desired capability and support the decision-making process, they are not a substitute for the process.

There are several other dimensions to the key steps leading to the decision to build an issues management function. As noted earlier, the emergence and recognition of a need is an implicit criticism of whatever capability or noncapability now exists. No matter how informal, unorganized, and undefined the current system is, information about the external world does get into the organization. Any new system will be far more successful if it recognizes, incorporates, and builds on the existing system than if it challenges, threatens, and competes with it or is seen as doing so.

To experienced senior management with long tenure in the organization, these existing systems and capabilities, along with the personnel comprising them, are so well known as to be second nature. Their contribution and value must be recognized and respected. For a relatively new member of the executive team, the existing system may be difficult to identify and appreciate. For this reason, the issues management advocate is often, but not always, an executive who has a great deal of experience and history with the organization (see the next section).

Another dimension is the secondary impacts of the process of building an issues management function. While the primary purpose is to improve the intelligence the organization is getting about its current and future operating environment, many secondary purposes may be served, depending on how the issues management function is realized. For example, it may be achieved by building up, formalizing, and overhauling an existing function that has not been assigned the generic mission of identifying and anticipating change. Or it may be built so as to bypass an existing system, allowing a CEO to put a personal stamp on the organization. It may be built to show the leadership of management in adopting a state-of-the-art concept and capability. An issues management function may be built as a home for a standing crisis management capability that, it is hoped, will rarely be used. Because of the possibility that those working on the endeavor may be distracted by issues irrelevant to the primary purpose, an awareness of the secondary impacts, intended or not, is essential in building an issues management function.

While most operating issues management functions do not have formal mission statements or goals, there is a well-established recognition of its goals and purposes both among those who direct and participate in the issues management function and within the general management. This sense of purpose and mission is essential, whether achieved by informal consensus or through carefully crafted statements. At the outset it is useful to have some written record of the purposes and goals of the issues management function. Of particular importance here are two factors: first, what the capability of the system is expected to be; and second, when it will reach that capability.

Because it takes several years to build a fully operational capability and the outlook on emerging issues over the interesting future is usually one covering several years, it is not credible to evaluate an issues management capability's output in the near term. It is, of course, valuable to evaluate the building of both the issues management process and organization in the near term.

The overriding goal of an issues management function is to enhance the current and long-term performance and standing of the corporation by anticipating change, promoting opportunities, and avoiding or mitigating threats. Attaining this corporate goal, of course, promotes the performance and standing of the corporate leadership, both within and outside the corporation, but this is secondary for issues management.

Just as issues management functions come in a variety of forms, they also serve this overriding objective through a variety of purposes and missions. While the six basic stages — scanning and issue detection, issue research and analysis, prioritizing, strategy development, implementation programs, and oversight — are present in all issues management functions, however formal or informal, their form is determined first and foremost by the purpose and mission of each particular issues management function.

THE NEED AND ROLE OF A CHAMPION

Most issues management functions are the result of the careful, sustained advocacy of a senior executive or group of senior executives. In many cases, this executive is a vice president of one of the strategic management units — corporate planning, government relations, public affairs, or public relations. The insight and vision of this individual or these individuals convince other senior executives to support the building of an issues management function.

There are two major kinds of issues management advocates. Usually, the advocate is someone with a long history in the organization and its top personnel. This advocate has a broad personal network throughout the organization and is well respected. Sometimes, however, the advocate is part of a new senior management team brought in after some crisis. The new management team or one of its members has acquired experience with issues management elsewhere and knows from personal experience of its value — especially in avoiding the kind of crisis that befell the previous management. The two kinds of advocates have one key element in common: they both must know well the styles and personalities of the senior management among whom the issues management function will operate in the future. While the processes outlined below apply to both circumstances, the pace of development for a new management team responding to an emergency is accelerated.

Some senior executives support the idea of issues management based on knowledge gained from the professional literature, others on personal experience with other organizations, others on the basis of watching competitors and listening to their networks. Still others find that necessity is still the mother of invention: they must respond to the pace of change, the sheer number of issues, the loss of control over their organization as external developments dominate and drive their organizations—the sense that events outside their organization have more of a say over its fate and future than they do.

A first step for the champion of the issues management concept is to become educated in the current state of the art of the field. As this is still a young, rapidly growing field, the professional literature is not well established. Several books have been written, but developments have moved rapidly along. Still, these books provide a valuable place to start and a view of the history of issues management.

Articles in professional journals provide a more current if less comprehensive view. Professional conferences, such as those offered annually by the Edison Electric Institute, the Issues Management Association, the Public Affairs Council, among others, provide information about the most recent developments in the field. For a list of issues management resources, networks, publications, and professional organizations, see the appendixes.

From an understanding developed from these resources, an executive can develop concepts of how internal issues move within the company, the industry, and the immediate environment. Though most of the public literature focuses on public issues, issues managers and corporate issues management functions must also be prepared to address what are for the most part internal private issues—private in the sense that these issues are specific to the company, its personnel, and its particular circumstances and do not reach a general audience, at least not initially.

PREPARING A DESIGN PROPOSAL

The issues management process offers a long-term return on investment. Moreover, the return will be difficult to measure: as history does not show the consequences of possible alternatives presented by the future, executives are left to opine and conjecture about what might have been. With a long-term subjective return, an issues management system must have strong high-level support for at least the time required to build and operate it and evaluate its performance. For a large, mature organization, this period is five years at a minimum. The level of effort, and hence of cost, will vary from corporation to corporation, but the time period will vary little.

For these reasons, a long-range design needs to be prepared. Depending on the nature of the organization, this may be of varying degrees of formality. Even in the most informal setting, it should be documented in writing. It may include an assessment of the need for the capability—at least as defined by forces in the external environment.

The design is built on a thorough understanding of the concepts of issues management as applied to the particular organization. This involves some research of current and applied issues management methods, resources, and capabilities. The link between the proposed issues management system and the existing strategic management process needs to be outlined to the extent practical. A schedule with appropriate milestones and oversight reviews must be included, along with assessments of anticipated problems and key decision points. Finally, the personnel and resources necessary are identified. When this proposal has been accepted by senior management, the building process can begin.[5]

DEFINING THE EXISTING SYSTEM

Machiavelli's axiom leads to the first essential principle: there is an old order — a way, a system or nonsystem, a means or method by which the corporation now accomplishes the issues management function. However badly it is done, it is being done. The corporation obtains information about current and emerging issues in its external environment — sooner or later. It may be unaware of an issue until the camera crews, issue advocates, and lawyers gather on the front lawn, but eventually it gets the message.

Obviously, this is an extreme example, but it has happened. With the continuing acceleration of the issues process, it will continue to happen, even to corporations with good issues management capabilities. The Tylenol people did not know about the tampering issue before it was all over the front page. Of course, the Tylenol killer could have selected any one of many food or over-the-counter drug products. Most manufacturers of similar products recognized this possibility and developed their own tammper-resistant packaging. Similarly, after the sudden-acceleration issue destroyed Audi's U.S. market, competing cars quietly installed interlocks to prevent the possibility of a copycat issue.

The existing issues management system may be no more than an informal ad hoc network of colleagues who, in addition to their formal responsibilities, serve as eyes and ears for the corporation, surfacing, and discussion issues in their daily work. This network may consist of executives in government relations, public affairs, planning, community relations, personnel, public relations, and communications or be centered in the mind of just one forward-looking executive. Its existence may not be obvious or even known to those interested in or assigned to developing a more formal issues management capability. Some research may be required to develop a complete picture of the existing capability. This is, however, a necessary first step to avoid unnecessary duplication and destructive turf battles.

Implicit in this early recognition of the need for faster, clearer, earlier intelligence on emerging issues is the recognition of some present capability, however minimal, unarticulated, disjointed, confused, and tardy it may be, for getting information about the changing environment into the organization. It is this capability or noncapability that needs to be analyzed, understood, and incorporated in the development of the more formal issues management function. Since there is an existing system, building an issues management capability necessarily involves organizational change. A first guiding principle is this:

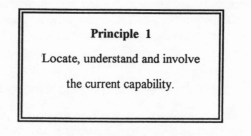

Principle 1

Locate, understand and involve

the current capability.

DEFINING THE PURPOSE

The second step is to understand the purposes and goals of the person or persons seeking to establish a new or more formal issues management capability. This understanding focuses on the impact any intervention will have both on the operation of the existing issues management capabilities and on the corporation as a whole. The purpose might include one or more of the following:

- To improve the existing capability
- To be recognized as being on the cutting edge of a most current management concept
- To bypass existing process and personnel
- To put a personal stamp on the corporation
- To improve early warning of threats and opportunities
- To organize standing response capability
- To have better current intelligence
- To institutionalize a personal capability, improving its long-range survivability
- To reduce risk and uncertainty
- To feel more confident about making decisions in the face of risk

A second guiding principle is:

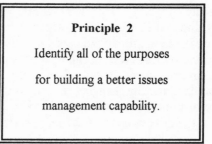

Principle 2

Identify all of the purposes

for building a better issues

management capability.

The decision to improve a corporation's issues management capability arises in response to the perception of a need. While the pace and power of emerging issues are usually the driving force creating this need, the decision to change the existing order is not likely to be seen by all as a prudent response to the changing environment of the corporation. Notwithstanding how clearly and carefully the need is defined, some part of the organization will see the decision to build a more formal issues management capability as criticism of its performance and a threat to its future. Even though an issues management function has not been previously defined and no individual or department has been assigned the responsibility, it is not difficult to understand how those who have been providing whatever limited issues management capability the corporation had might well believe it is their responsibility to accomplish the issues management function or major parts of it. At a very minimum, if a greater capability is needed, they would — or should — have identified the need first.

This is just human nature. "This is my idea, issue, concept, role, or whatever. Who says you can mess with it?" It is just this human behavior that keeps issue management systems from ever doing anything about an issue without clear directions from the highest authority.

From the human dynamics of change in a mature organization, the earliest presentation of the idea for change must be handled with appropriate tact and skill. It is essential that those most directly affected by any change be included in the decision process from the start. This is why defining the existing capability and identifying the players in it are so important. Thus principle number three is:

Principle 3

Don't start from scratch:

Build onto the existing capability.

THE PACE OF CHANGE: FOUR PITFALLS

When the mission of a greater or improved issues management capability is defined, there is often a desire to try to fill this need quickly. This leads to four common pitfalls:

- Fast cats
- Copy cats
- Fat cats
- Black cats

Fast Cats. Builders of issues management systems do not fail because they move too slowly but because they move too fast. Depending on the nature of the corporation, a good benchmark is to plan to spend a year walking around and gaining familiarity with the existing capabilities and personalities, while familiarizing them with the plans for change. During this time, it is essential to survey how key persons now stay in touch with the changing view of the future, to make an inventory of recent, current, and likely emerging issues, as well as their ownership within the corporation, and to inventory current sources used to anticipate change. In these surveys, it is important to solicit as many inputs as possible and circulate all results.

In general, it is better at this stage to focus money, time, and resources on building the process rather than producing products. It is best to grow the capability in the four stages of issues management — scanning, prioritizing, researching, and developing candidate strategies, one at a time. In short, the fourth principle is this:

Principle 4

Patience. Build slowly:

No fast cats.

Copy Cats. To avoid this slow growing process, it is tempting to try to move more rapidly by copying the capability developed by another corporation. An issues management system can be seen as consisting of both hardware and software. As with computers, issues management hardware is the physical part — the files, data bases, scanning resources, issue briefs, and the like. How these are used — the design of the system and how it operates — is the software. While much can be borrowed in nature of hardware, it must be carefully adapted to the personality and personnel of each corporation: it must develop its own software. While a copycat capability may look like it is working in the near term, the mismatch will soon become apparent to all. A fifth principle, then, is this:

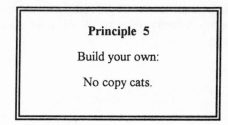

Principle 5

Build your own:

No copy cats.

Fat Cats. Another short-cut to the building process that those with fat budgets have tried is to buy a capability via one or more of the services offering trend analysis, emerging issues, forecasting services, publications, focus groups, roundtables, and the like. Such broadcast services, which offer the same product or service to many different clients, have several inevitable limitations: first, they cannot cover in any depth the issues particular to a corporation or even industry; second, because they are no more than large, generic scanning systems themselves, the information they produce is necessarily out of date by the time it passes through their internal processing cycle.

The broadcast services provided by recognized firms do, however, have at least one built-in advantage: they carry a certain amount of credibility and reputation with them. At the very minimum, they can serve as key checkpoints for the output of a corporation's own developing scanning system. Some specialized scanning systems, such as CongresScan™ or Duke Merriam's *Issues Management Letter,* provide access to resources that would not otherwise be available and cannot be duplicated internally. Others, such as Mike Marion's *FutureSurvey,* published by the World Future Society, provide a broad scan of a variety of resources that no single issues management system could expect to cover independently. (See Chapter 5 for a listing of other resources.) While these broadcast services have a role to play, it is a limited one of being input to an in-house issues management capability, not a substitution for it. The sixth principle is simply this:

Principle 6

Build. Don't buy:

No fat cats.

INTELLIGENCE VS. OPERATIONS:
DON'T "JUST DO SOMETHING"

Black Cats. Finally, a word of caution—again. Among the major design questions, is that of what the issues management capability will do with the information it generates. There is a natural human urge to "do something" about the future needs of the corporation. In the intelligence community, "doing something" is called a black operation. This urge must be resisted totally and completely.

Even if the new issues management system has been carefully built with no ability or authority to "do something," the need to justify its existence will eventually arise. Even if this were a good course—and it is not—there are great dangers ahead. There are only three kinds of issues facing the corporation: first, those that some person or department feels it already "owns"; second, those that everybody and every department has been able to push into the space between the boxes; and third, those that the issues management system has identified before anyone else.

The issues management department cannot touch any issue already owned by any other part of the organization without great trouble. This choice produces extremely high, prompt mortality. Machiavelli had it right. It can have all the orphan issues—the ones all other departments have successfully ducked. Those who would like to see the issues management system fail are more than willing to play "let Mikie try it." What better way to knock off the new kid on the block than to demonstrate the futility of this new idea? If these issues were not losers for whoever touches them, they would not be orphans.

Finally, there are the totally new, as yet unowned issues. As noted before, these will be highly subjective, based on hunches, guesswork, assumptions, conjecture, or worse. The vast majority of such issues will never grow to the most embryonic stage, and any effort spent on them is most likely to look, at best, foolish and naive.

The best model for an issues management system is that described earlier, that of the corporation's chief financial officer, who—though keeper of the purse—has no general authority to spend the corporation's funds. The general conservatism and caution traditionally associated with this function are also parts of a good model.

For these reasons, an issues management system should have no general authority to respond to any of the information it generates. It is an intelligence function that rigorously avoids even the potential of the possibility of the appearance of meddling in the operations side. It only provides information—and recommendations, if asked—to the authorized leadership which will determine what is to be done and who will do it. Resources of the issues management capability may or may not be used, but it is involved only when specifically authorized. If the issues management capability has any general authority, other parts of the corporation will always fear that issues management might negate their best-laid plans. The seventh principle is this:

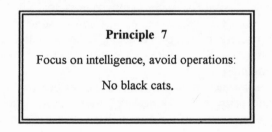

Principle 7

Focus on intelligence, avoid operations:

No black cats.

A summary of these principles is provided in Figure 7.1.

GETTING STARTED: WALK-ABOUT

The process of building an issues management capability begins with some awareness that the corporation could and needs to perform better than it

Figure 7.1
Issues Management Construction Principles: Summary

1

Locate, understand and involve
the current capability.

2

Identify all of the purposes
for building a better issues
management capability.

3

Don't start from scratch:
Build onto the existing capability.

4

Patience. Build slowly:
No fast cats.

5

Build your own:
No copy cats.

6

Build. Don't buy:
No fat cats.

7

Focus on intelligence, avoid operations:
No black cats.

---

currently is in the issues process. This perception recognizes, as noted earlier, that some system or nonsystem, however indifferent or disorganized, now exists. Information about the external world does penetrate into the strategic management of every corporation. In the late 1960s, the leaders of General Motors learned about its immediate external environment when they watched downtown Detroit burn from their corporate office towers. However belatedly, the news does eventually penetrate. The existing system or order must be recognized and respected.

The first step depends on who in the organization recognizes this need. If it is an executive authorized to initiate a new program in this area, all the better. If not, the first task is identifying and reaching this person.

How this person is approached and briefed is a matter of the culture of the organization. At a minimum, those advocating a more formal issues management capability must assess the current capability, system, or nonsystem. They must also prepare some background information on the issues management process, capability, resources, alternate designs, the work of others, and so on. With the appropriate authorization, an organized effort to review the potential of an issues management may be undertaken.

Occasionally, the need is obvious to many executives at once, often because of some crisis inside or outside the corporation that is generally recognized and believed to have been avoidable had some better system been available. In this case, a more formal decision to evaluate the value of issues management will be made.

The next steps are somewhat independent and can be undertaken in any order or simultaneously. Some understanding of the existing internal system must be developed. Who are the leaders? Where are they located? How do they report, present, or inject ideas about emerging issues into the strategic management process and the corporation's consciousness? What resources do they use?

From the external world, some understanding of the principles of issues management is required from both a public policy and an issues development cycle perspective and as a management process. This external information gathering and research need not initially be deeply involved. There are many informal issues management networks that can be accessed. Most industry and professional associations have some knowledge of and access to these networks. At a minimum, they are part of the American Society of Association Executives' (ASAE) network. Professional associations in the field, such as the Issues Management Association, the Public Affairs Section of the Public Relations Society of America, the International Public Relations Association, the Issues Network, the Professional Section of the World Futures Society, among others, have networks that can be accessed.

Another category of information to be gathered concerns the various resources the different issues management programs use. These include books, professional journals, articles, consulting organizations and individuals, scanning resources, and other sources. An initial list of these is presented in the appendixes.

At these early stages, word will spread about the new idea, about change. Suspicion and fear will spread. What are they up to now? Who is doing this? What are they doing? How will it affect me? My issues? My plans? My career? My budget?

In a sense, this is the first issue the issues management function must address. It can only be addressed head-on: all information about the issues management function, plans, and potential operations must be made available to all concerned parties within the corporation. If there is one thing that is well established in organizational change, it is that secrecy is highly destructive, very expensive, and counterproductive. Winslow's law sums it up best:[7]

Secrecy is the fertilizer of entropy.

To avoid fertilizing entropy, the issues management design and concept need to be walked throughout the current senior management and those who plan to join senior management in the future. While the planning sessions for the design and schedule of the issues management function need not be "public" to the senior management, all meetings of the issues management group must be. To keep the group effective and efficient, the group should be small: only a few at first, never growing to more than twelve to fifteen attendees at a time. Some corporations have a larger roster so the normal meeting size is in this range. However, any senior manager or his or her designate may attend the meetings as observers.

An open door policy is essential. Once the procedures and methods are common knowledge, the fear and suspicion will fade. The sense of threat will abate. Concern and attention will turn to another topic. Key to this is a slow, evolutionary process with appropriate organizational checks and balances. With an issues process that relies on existing organizational bodies to evaluate the issues, develop alternatives, and plan strategies, the fear of a loose cannon will never develop.

As important as the design characteristics are in providing this sense of security, the personnel involved are even more important. The leader who walks the design about must be of the corporate culture, a well-known commodity, a trusted, accessible team player. Obviously, this cannot be an outsider, a transfer, a new employee—other than a new CEO. While supporting external technical expertise can be used or hired, control of the operation as perceived by those in senior management who might be concerned must remain in the hand of this trusted insider.

The schedule of the walk-about is often a year or more. A couple of months before the first meeting of the I/M group, the walk-about should begin. It continues through the first cycle of the process or until all interested parties have lost interest and accepted issues management as a necessity.

THE LINK TO STRATEGIC PLANNING

The traditional strategic planning process grew from long-range planning. These processes usually followed annual cycles, often with well-defined steps and stages. The difference between long-range planning and strategic planning is more than semantics, though there is no settled definition for this difference. At a minimum, strategic planning is a broader, more holistic, comprehensive, and inclusive analysis of the longer-term future. Where long-range planning might be described as seeking to optimize current lines of business, strategic planning would begin with a focus on how changing dynamics of the external world will effect the purpose and need of customers of the current lines of business.

Another definition is the old addage, "Long-range planning seeks to do the job right; strategic planning seeks to do the right job." Clearly, the operating assumptions are quite different. Long-range planning has an internal focus, while strategic planning expressly includes the external world. If a corporation does not explicitly include changes in the external world in its long-range process—if its process is more akin to long-range planning—then linking issues management will be more difficult. It will, however, still follow the concepts outlined later for a more strategic planning process.

There are at least four stages to strategic planning:

1. Identifying the topics to be included
2. Developing forecasts for each topic
3. Selecting goals for each topic
4. Identifying strategies for each goal

Identifying topics is the key step. The assumptions made at this point, the breadth and scope of the entire process, are defined at this point. While the importance of each of the stages is equal in terms of their interrelated roles, the additional importance of this stage in defining the entire process promotes it to preeminent importance.

At this stage, the balance between internal and external topics will also be set. Even the most narrowly defined scope, one limited to internal topics only, will not be able to ignore the external world of emerging issues. The forecasting stage will not be complete without forecasts that explicitly consider potential external surprises that will change the assumptions and forecasts of each topic. The formal forecasting methods addressing surprise events include cross-impact analysis, trend impact analysis, probabilistic systems dynamics, and policy impact analysis. If nothing more, the issues management process will identify potential surprises for use in these advanced forecasting processes.

A more balanced approach will use the results of the scanning stages of issues management to identify candidate topics for inclusion in the first stage of the forecasting process. Many corporations maintain parallel tracks of internal and external issues, while others combine them in a single track. Eventually, the two are integrated into one, with advantages to both early and late integration. The process of selecting topics for inclusion is difficult under the best of circumstances. As with the issues management process itself, the key to this selection process is informed judgment. However, executives find it most difficult to be informed without some forecasts, without knowing some of the potential surprises, without knowing some of the cross-impacts of external events. This is a chicken-and-egg problem. Early integration helps to some degree. On the other hand, early integration inevitably shifts the orientation of the strategic planning process inward. External issues become defined in terms of their impact on internal ones, and independent evaluation becomes impossible. Broad, sweeping issues that may redefine the entire operating environment of part or all of a corporation's future can easily be missed.

The selection process is accomplished through a variety of methods. From brainstorming to formal group processing techniques such as Delphi, participants in the strategic planning process apply selection criteria. Typically, these criteria include importance, probability, impact positive (opportunity) vs. impact negative (threat), foreseeability, reversibility, ability to influence, authority to influence, expectations of the many corporate publics (customers, suppliers, employees, regulators), cost of opportunity, risk, and so on. These criteria are applied in their order of generality, the most general being first.

In the final stages, complex and compound evaluations may be used. Compound evaluations allow the participants to weight their opinions by an independent factor, such as level of expertise, knowledge, responsibility, familiarity, or even management rank. Complex evaluations use the same criteria but apply them to individual parts, operations, mission, functions, products, or divisions of the corporation. The final evaluation of each topic is the sum of these individual evaluations.

Such complex evaluations allow for greater detail, identifying places where impacts will fall. This leads to the development of strategies focused not on single issues, topics, or forecasts but on departments, missions, functions, or operations. It enriches the entire process. By separating positive and negative impacts, executives can identify strategies that enhance the desirable impacts and mitigate undesirable ones.

In this process, the external topics from the issues management process are carried forward at the same level of attention and development as internal ones. This equality assures a balance between the two perspectives.

OVERSIGHT AND REVIEW

Because an issues management capability necessarily has a long-term mission, its evaluation must also be in the long term. If it takes one to two years to grow this capability, it cannot be evaluated for several years. Although its growth can and should be evaluated along the way, determining whether the capability is fulfilling its mission must wait until it has been established and had an opportunity to build a track record. In other words, while the capability is being built, unpleasant surprises will probably still occur—that you are building a capability does not mean that you yet have one. Even after the capability is in place, unpleasant surprises will still occur; but their frequency, suddenness, and severity will decline.

There are initially two dimensions to evaluate and review. First, is the design and its implementation. Is it on schedule? Is it on budget? Are the performance milestones being met? Is an issues management system building a network of supporters and users? Second, is the system beginning to work as it evolves? Are issues being anticipated at earlier points than would have otherwise occurred? Is the response of the organization to its changing environment improving and developing some clarity, purpose, and vision?

These are highly subjective criteria. The few crude objective criteria seem totally inadequate, more focused and limited to input characteristics and macroscopic dimensions than to output performance. However, the absence of objective measures does not mean subjective ones should not be used. They will be used—the only question is whether they will be explicitly and formally recognized or left to the organization's collective subconscious. Clearly, an orderly, open, explicit process holds the best prospects for the long-term performance of the issues management system.

One of the characteristics that successful corporations have in common is their ability to anticipate and capitalize on change. Although it is not an easy task, it is one of ever growing value.

8

Major Issues Management Design Alternatives

There are many design alternatives for an issues management function. Each corporation's process and design is really unique, even when one appears to be identical to another on paper. The written description and charts are only our best efforts in summarizing a highly organic, personal process. The translation of these inert words and lines into action will be different for each corporation.

There are, however, several major categories of design alternatives. These are discussed in this chapter.

THE COMMITTEE SYSTEM

Admittedly, the idea of yet another committee is not attractive. However unpopular the name might be, committees can be effective means of operating an issues management system, particularly if the conduct of the meetings is subject to a little discipline.

Typically, the committee is assembled over a year or two by the I/M group leader. Though there is a natural human drive to involve the highest-level management available, this is usually not the most important criterion. The senior management will already participate in the issues management function through the annual strategic planning process. This is the stage for the evaluation of issues and development of strategy. This senior strategic management process will develop directions and specific-issue action strategies that the I/M committee will support.

The primary function of the committee is to identify and anticipate emerging issues. It is to gather intelligence on the future and alternate futures. It has an outlook focused on the interesting future—that point when the major strategy and policy options of today begin to change the course of the corporation (see Chapter 1). This time frame is often several years into the future. Hence, those who sit on the committee today should be those expected to occupy leadership positions when these issues arise. This assures that the issues will not be a hypothetical exercise but one of vital importance to the executives themselves.

As with the issues management leader, these additional assignments of participating in issues management should not be left to the generosity of the individual executive. Issues management should be incorporated into the job descriptions of all who are tapped to participate in it.

THE PROFESSIONAL STAFF

Initially, the leader of the issues management group will be the senior executive described earlier. He or she will have one or more other primary tasks. Issues management will not begin as an exclusive assignment but may well become one. As the I/M process develops, the executive leader will need the support of those skilled in various aspects of the issues management process—scanning, networking, issues research, information system design, group decision techniques, and the like. These are added as the need arises. Often, the first professional added to the issues management group is someone skilled in issues research. At the early stages, this may be an experienced research librarian who knows the literature and informational resources needed to support issues research. If senior management has a speech writer, he or she may be brought in to support the issues research.

Eventually, a professional will be added to the issues management staff to research the emerging issues identified by the I/M group. Over the start-up period, several professionals might be added. It is important to remember that these are research and information resource support personnel, they are not a substitute for the participation of the future executive leaders.

These issues research and information resource people will have a wide variety of backgrounds, from law to literature, library science to technical sciences, political science to policy analysis, public relations to public policy planning. Many will have advanced degrees. All of them bring their own issues network and resources to the team. They can be expected to be or become members of the various issues management networks across a wide spectrum.

MATRIX MODEL

To assure a wide scope of input, the executives who participate in the issues management process need to reflect the range of interests of the corporation. While the senior leadership in a corporate headquarters may be able to meet this requirement, it is virtually certain that they will not see emerging issues as quickly and as clearly as those who first encounter them. For this reason, members of the issues management group are often drawn from across the organization in all major dimensions—organizationally, geographically, divisionally—in the style of the matrix management concept. This assures the richest flow of emerging issues information.

The issues management group is often a two-tiered system, with a core group in the corporate headquarters working with a network of scanners in a matrix model. While the core group will meet quarterly or as needed for rapidly breaking developments, the matrix network of scanners might meet annually to review their work, scanning resources, and new ideas. The American Council of Life Insurance, in its trends assessment program, pioneered this model in the early 1970s under the direction of Eddie Weiner and Arnold Brown. The United Way national headquarters convenes its environmental scanning committee twice a year. These conventions of participants keep the group identified, focused, and networking. It is an essential part of the maintenance of a scanning system.

SELECTING THE I/M PARTICIPANTS

The success of an issues management process depends on its first stage, the scanning of the external and internal environment for potential emerging issues. While this does not seem like a complex or involved process, building a successful scanning system is one of the most difficult tasks, in part because of the nature of our culture. Executives who reach the senior ranks do so because they meet or exceed some particular standards of accuracy, dependability, reliability, caution, level-headedness, stability, patience, clarity, singleness of purpose, and the like. We reward executives who solve problems much more than those who avoid them.

This standard almost requires these characteristics of executives if they are to advance. In the converse, they must not be distracted and act on the basis of incomplete information or, worse, mere speculation about *possible* future issues. They must never embrace uncertainty but consider a wide range of factors not specifically within their area of responsibility. Incentives are not structured to encourage an executive to engage in high-risk behavior with few rewards. With plenty of opportunities for heroics in fighting existing fires, only the most dedicated executive would sacrifice his or her efforts in fire prevention.

Yet it is these most dedicated who must be found to participate in the issues management group. The perspective of potential issues must be broad, and many corporations deliberately seek the participation of executives across the organizational chart. The key characteristic is not necessarily the one that leads to the senior executive position. Described in many different ways, this characteristic is found in those few people who, with no obvious effort, always seem to know of a broad range of developments, issues, and subjects well beyond their specialty, educational background, current or former assignments. Sometimes called gate-keepers, network-nodes, and renaissance men or women, such people have a unique ability to see and sense emerging issues.

Speculation among leaders in the field focuses on the theory of right-brain dominance among these renaissance people. If right-brain dominance does play a role and if current theory that women are more likely to be right-brain dominant is correct, then women should be expected to excel at this function. While no scientific study has yet been made of this theory, experience in the field has shown women usually are much better at keeping informed across a broad spectrum of issues than men. The early and continuing leadership and success of women in issues management in general, and the Issues Management Association in particular, bear this out.

While the senior executive selected to organize and lead the issues management function is, on the basis of demographics, more likely to be a man, the history of the leadership and success of women executives in issues management requires that a special effort be made to assure the valuable and significant contributions that women executives, including some very young ones, are capable of making.

9

Growing Issues Management into the Organization

Organizational change is a lengthy process that needs continuous reinvention. The techniques and concepts that worked today will not work tomorrow. The issues management function of the original design must be continuously readapted to the changing needs and cultural environment of the corporation. For these reasons, growing issues management into the organization is an on-going process. While an issues management system can be built in as little as a year, it will take several cycles—and therefore, years—for it to become fully operational, valuable and contributing. To reach maturity, having most of its organizational roots and connections, takes three to five years.

LINKAGES TO OTHER MANAGEMENT FUNCTIONS

Through the annual strategic planning process, the issues management function will begin to build its organizational links. First of these, usually, are the links to the public issues process, policy planning function, public affairs functions, and community and employee relations offices. As issues are identified for issue action strategies, these offices and functions are most likely to be involved along with the substantive line department leadership.

The issues management group does not have a leadership role on an issue action team. The line management that first identified the emerging issue has the right of first refusal for this position. If it declines, the position normally goes to the line management with the most at stake. For large issues cutting across the corporation, a multimember steering group may be needed.

In any event, the issue action leader assembles the needed resources from within the corporate staff, tapping the issues management group for its issues research capabilities — for example, the public affairs office for its public opinion intelligence or the government relations office for the latest on legislative trends.

As the experience with the issues management process grows, the number of departments involved in issue action teams will grow. The network of support staff to the team will often involve many of the same players — the leadership and staff of public affairs, community relations, stockholder relations, government relations, and corporate planning.

It is a growing task of the issues management group to keep the institutional memory of its issue action team members, methods, successes, and failures. As new issues arise, the issues management leadership will know the corporation's best human and organizational resources. This valuable leadership function can only be accomplished by developing and growing personal contacts and networks across the corporation.

EXPANDING THE I/M FOCUS: BUILDING AN AUDIENCE

The idea of publishing and distributing lists of emerging issues, issue papers, or issue briefs is frequently greeted with significant suspicion and outright skepticism. Isn't this proprietary information? Won't outsiders, even enemies, get this and use it against us? What if government regulators get it? Or our competitors? Clearly, they will. But that does not have to be a problem. The key to this dilemma is in the definition of the "it" in these fears.

It does no damage to a corporation if the whole world discovers it recognizes AIDS as a major problem for its employees, its customers, and the financial security of not just health care systems but the country; or that it is concerned about national and international transborder data flow restrictions; or that it recognizes the special problems involved in trade with some countries. Issue papers are not position papers. They do not include even a discussion of strategy options. They are background papers designed to educate the reader about the current status and likely future of an issue that may be important to the future of the corporation. Issue briefs educate, inform, and sensitize the reader. They invite the reader's own thoughts, suggestions, possible impacts, new ideas, the latest developments.

While the circulation is always open, the number of copies and their distribution grows as the issues management function grows. Initially, as outlined in Chapter 6, these issue papers usually circulate at the highest level until the leadership at this level is sufficiently comfortable to allow broader circulation. Eventually, the content of the issues papers, if not the papers themselves, circulates throughout the corporation. Keeping the papers in the open domain prevents the growth of suspicion, secrecy, and the adverse consequences of Winslow's Law: Secrecy is the fertilizer of entropy.

I/M's FIRST PRODUCTS

To facilitate the participation of senior executives and promote communication on emerging issues, scanning newsletters or scans are often circulated among senior management even before the first issue paper has been prepared. This need not be a large responsibility, but it usually is a formal one. A very modest support staff is also usually needed to organize and maintain the scanning system.

A good model for these scan newsletters is difficult to find. The vice president of futures research at Security Pacific National Bank, Hank Koehn, prepared what were at the time the standards by which all other scan newsletters were measured. While Koehn did not have a formula, some characteristics of his work that contributed to his success can be identified. Balance was clearly one. Though writing for a large financial institution, Koehn never let financial issues dominate. He covered the waterfront for any issues that might be important, from recreational drugs, to an aging population, to new technologies for personal identification.

Koehn also brought an optimistic perspective. Never ducking a problem or threat, Koehn always found the silver lining or an angle for the lighter side if not out right humor. "If you can imagine it, you can do it" was his philosophy. He was not afraid to use cartoons to get heavy points across. He varied the focus, from macroissues on the global scale to always something for the little guy. He always applied the KISS principle—Keep It Simple, Stupid! His scans were rarely more than a few sentences.

As his external audience was so large, he did not have the capability to make his scan newsletter a two-way communication, but this is ideal. Every internal scan newsletter should invite reader participation in every issue. Not just the chestnut, "Call us if you have any ideas," but a survey, a question, a specific request for ideas on an issue or comments on an idea. Regular reporting of responses will assure participation and develop the audience. Also, a scan newsletter will build audiences for the issue papers that follow.

As the issues management function grows, the scan newsletter will grow in formality, format, and editorial review. To the extent possible, ossification is to be resisted. The scan newsletter should be a little irreverent, a little daring, innovative, and willing to air the lighter side of popular myths and myth-makers.

ISSUES NEWSLETTERS

Issues newsletters are a natural outgrowth of scan newsletters, but they are much more difficult to produce. While some large corporations have such newsletters, they are more common among associations. The American Council of Life Insurance pioneered this idea with its *Straws in the Wind*. The Congressional Clearinghouse for the Future publishes *What's Next?*

The American Society of Mechanical Engineers publishes *The ASME Issues Management Newsletter*. No doubt there are many more. The production of such a newsletter, however, is not necessarily a goal of an issues management function, unless the corporation's size and scope so indicate.

COMMUNICATING WITH PUN AND PUNCH:
ISSUE CARTOONS

Cartoons are funny, even silly, immature, for kids, not serious—at least not serious enough to have any place in the work of *professional* issue managers. Or do cartoons have a place?

Lincoln had an idea that applies here: On the emancipation of the slaves he said, "As our case is new, so our argument must be new." Though cartoons do not often have a role in other professions, this alone is no reason to bar them from use when they have an important role to play in the purposes of a new profession. In identifying, communicating, and exploring emerging issues—major purposes of issues management—issue cartoons offer several unique advantages.

Cartoons communicate tremendous amounts of information quickly, efficiently, and—if the humor is good—memorably. A picture speaks to the right-brain, offering relief from the tedium of left-brain, linear analyses. Worth more than mere words—even a thousand of them—a good cartoon invites a thousand interpretations, challenging executives and other users to be creative and imaginative.

By leaving so much for the individual to do, a single cartoon can stimulate a group to a full range of possible impacts of an issue. Since these ideas come from the group, they are likely to be more permanent than those suggested by outsiders and others. Also, only those familiar with an organization can see the real implications of an issue for their particular organization: analyses prepared by others for general distribution, however good, cannot match the richness, context, and "fit" a group of senior leaders is able to provide. Certainly, good left-brain analyses can help executives to be creative and make the fit: it is the cartoon, however, that virtually requires that they do so. Little wonder that it is quite common to find issue cartoons decorating offices, newsletters, and bulletin boards.

Cartoons are "hat racks for thoughts"—executives can hang a lot of ideas on a single cartoon—and with the cartoon, they have a place to keep many ideas without the necessity of remembering all the details. In the hat rack role, cartoons allow executives to continuously update, reinterpret, and explore new dimensions of issues every time they think about them.

Most important, cartoons allow an organization to handle through humor issues too difficult, painful, controversial, or dangerous to handle any other way; executives can communicate ideas that they can't, shouldn't, or don't want to verbalize.

Cartoons from major national publications say two important things about the issue: at least the editor is on the record as believing the issue has reached a national scale—i.e., the cartoon will be seen and understood across the country (or world). Moreover, national public opinion has reached a consensus that the subject of the cartoon has become an issue. There may be little or no consensus on the resolution of an issue, but there is consensus that it is an issue—or so one editor thinks. National cartoons provide an escape from the trap of a perspective dominated by local media, attitudes, and other parochialisms.

Of course, an editor can be wrong. There is perhaps no greater signal of an issue than an issues cartoon that does not make sense or one that appears off the mark or in poor taste or otherwise inappropriate. Such a cartoon means either the user is not current on the area of concern, much less the issue, or not in touch with mainstream attitudes. Such an extremely important signal calls for immediate research and resolution.

Scanning cartoons gives an executive a great deal of leverage: in selecting the fifteen to twenty cartoons for each issue of the *New Yorker,* for example, the editor reviews more than two thousand candidates. On average, only three issue cartoons are presented—the rest are pure fun.[1]

Cartoons have become so popular, the media have begun to feature them. In 1984 the *New York Times* added a summary of weekly issue cartoons to its Sunday "Week in Review" section. In 1985, the *Washington Post* added a similar summary to its Saturday op-ed page. The *Washington Times* includes a similar summary in its Sunday edition. In 1987, the Public Broadcasting Service's *MacNeil/Lehrer News Hour* added a cartoon section to its closing. And, of course, for many years *The World Press Review* has presented a summary of cartoons from around the world. Recently, the *New York Times* presented a review of Soviet issue and political cartoons, not from the underground but from the established press, including two biting satirical pokes at Russian leadership published in *Pravda.*[2]

The power of issue cartoons reached the general public when Attorney General Edwin Meese fired his press officer over a cartoon. The cartoon in question showed Reagan reading a horoscope and asking Meese, "What's your sign?" The second box showed Meese holding a sign that read "For Sale."[3] The media attacks on Dan Quayle became so common that Quayle jokes began to spread. Eventually, Johnny Carson began to pick on Quayle. The media finally took notice of the importance of becoming a joke on the Carson show almost a decade after Carson had lamented the impending defeat of Carter, noting he would have to go back to work for material—it would no longer be handed to him.[4] Surely, the issue cartoon has come of age.

For all these reasons—and just for fun—cartoons are a tool issues managers can use with great effect. They have earned a place and play a most valuable communications role in the early stages of the issues identification process.

PART IV

The Evolving Issues Process

10

The Issues Media

GROWTH OF "COMPUNICATIONS" TECHNOLOGIES

The technology of the information environment has changed so rapidly in the past two decades it is difficult to keep pace. Some analysts believe the changes brought on by the integrated computer chip and its children—large-scale integrated circuit (LSIC), very LSIC, and very high-speed integrated circuit (VHSIC)—to be so profound that history will be divided into before and after chip—BC and AC. These chips take their form in ever more sophisticated processing circuits, backed by larger and larger read-only and random-access memories—ROMs and RAMs. Other commentators find the merger of computers with the new communications technologies of satellites, laser fiber optics, laser or compact disks, and ISDN (Integrated Services, Digital Networks) to coin a new word: *compunications*. Similarly, the infrastructure of these technologies becomes *infostructure*.

The first million-transistor chip came on the market in the spring of 1989. An entire PC of what would have been "large" capacity a decade ago now fits on a single chip. Just ten years ago, the first word processor cost $17,000, used 9-inch 60-page disks, had 64,000 bytes of memory, and weighed more than 120 pounds. By 1984, a similar capability cost $3,000, used 5-(-inch 100-page disks, had twice the memory, and weighed 40 pounds. Today, all that technology and more fits into a 4-pound laptop with three to four million units of memory and 3½-inch 300-page disks—for less than $1000. That is a 17-to-1 price ratio in current dollars.

For comparison, the computer on the Space Shuttle, a design that was "frozen" in the mid-1970s, has a 250K of memory—puny by today's technology. Of course, two decades ago, such a capability would have filled a small house, requiring both continuous refrigeration and maintenance.

Figure 10.1
Computer Calculations per Dollar, 1955 to 2005

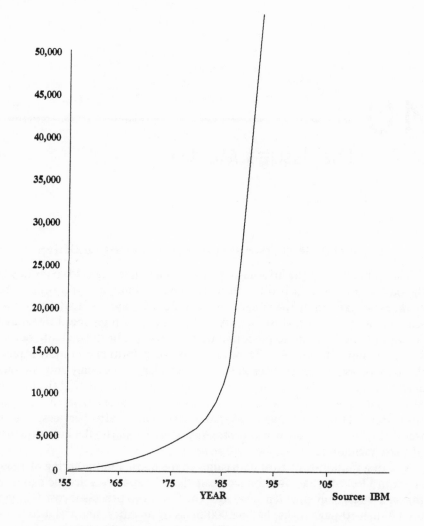

"Computer time" on a mainframe then cost more than $1,000 per hour, and no one could afford to use it merely for word processing. The dimensions of the revolution in computers can be seen in the number of computer calculations produced per dollar over the last 30 years, shown in Figure 10.1. The combinations of compactness, low cost, low energy, and extremely high reliability fueled the revolution. It is not too surprising that PC sales reached more than eleven million units in 1989—up by a factor of seventeen over 1981.

There is not an industry that has not been radically reformed by the power of this curve. Indeed, today 47 percent of the labor force is working in information industries or services.[1] A sense of the impact of this curve can be seen in its impact in one highly visible industry—passenger aircraft. Before computers, aircraft were designed to uniform stress loads—typically, a design factor of five to seven times the normal load was used. (The B-29, which first flew in 1943, was the last plane designed by hand.) After a certain number of flying hours, the structure was presumed to have weakened or become fatigued so much that it would have to be rebuilt or replaced.

With the first computers (and some experience from the field), aeronautical engineers could identify and design to different stress loads. For example, a wing might need to withstand three times as much up stress as down. Thus, the various components could be designed to their particular loads. Still, a design had a fixed life.

The first microcomputers allowed still more sophisticated analyses of loads and designs. For the first time, however, computers were compact enough to be taken on board to measure the actual stresses experienced by each individual structure over its life. Rather than a fixed number of hours, the structure's life would depend on its unique history, its actual fatigue.

The next generation of computers allowed for on-board control systems to manage the stresses on the aircraft as it flew, so that fatigue due to stress could be reduced, further extending the life of the structure. Such active control systems appeared in the early 1970s on the DC-10 and L1011.

The older Boeing aircraft that recently had in-flight structural failures—and thus gave us more experience from the field—were all first-generation computer designs—747s and 737s with major components designed in the 1950s. Moreover, none of these failures were due to any extraordinary stress loads of the moment such as might be generated by turbulence, but came during normal stresses that were too much for the fatigue generated over the life of the aircraft.

This obviously raises serious questions about maintenance, inspection, and repair capabilities. More important, it raises questions about the design standards of these first jets and computer-aided load-specific design philosophies. And with that, we have not even come to concerns about the two generations of aircraft that were designed by engineers who assumed the validity of earlier design philosophies and used the increased computer technologies to go well beyond primitive load-specific philosophies.

The dramatic changes so visible in aircraft hardware, performance, costs, and systems are easily rivaled by those in the traditional information media, though they are not as visible and tangible. Compunication technologies have brought as profound an impact on society (if not more profound) by revolutionizing the traditional information media, albeit by more subtle means. In virtually every dimension, the change has been so great as to define a "sea change."

Compare the TV viewer of 1969 with one today: the three, real-time synchronous-network choices have expanded, with cable and satellites, to choices of 50, 100, or more channels. In addition, with the same basic TV (now color in 93 percent of homes, half with commercial-dodging remote control), the viewer today can also select from several public and educational networks, HBO movies, dedicated themes via CNN, MTV, ESPN, C-SPAN, and so on. In 80 percent of homes, asynchronous viewing on a VCR of tapes from personal collections, various private sources, and public libraries is also possible.

The prerecorded VCR tape industry, which sold 5 million copies in 1981, sold an estimated 93 million in 1989. This growth in sales would no doubt have been much larger except for the illegal counterfeiting that can be easily accomplished with readily available commercial VCRs. With both VCR tapes and computer software, the technological challenge to the copyright laws has been so profound that most suppliers make no more than a cursory effort at protection—the obligatory recital of penalties, but little more. Indeed, most once proprietary software is now in the domain of "shareware"—and tapes are headed in the same direction.

The target of advertising, once so easy to reach, is now highly elusive in an increasingly decentralized, supplier-and-technology-competitive "info-tainment" market. Moreover, those with greater disposable incomes are even harder to reach, using ever more technology to follow their particular information and entertainment interests, which rarely include the "vast waste-land" of commercial TV. This view of the wired world does not even include any of the other current and near-term emerging technologies such as Camcorders, laser video disks, and visual information systems (VIS), much less any of the more speculative technologies of the not too distant future.

This decentralization of the traditional information media is not limited to the electronic media. The daily newspaper has seen a similar trend. The number of smaller newspapers (circulation under 50,000) is up 51 percent since 1985 while the number with more than 250,000 circulation is down 26 percent. According to the American Newspaper Publishers Association, circulation of major urban dailies is off 16 percent in the past decade, a more striking decline when viewed against a simultaneous 20 percent growth in the number of households. Meanwhile, the circulation of suburban weeklies has grown 50 percent, from half the total circulation of dailies to more than 75 percent today. Given the demographics, politics, and relative incomes of the older urban dailies and the newer suburbs, the implications for the future are clear.

For those who prefer to pursue the commercial aspects of TV, there are growing numbers of TV catalogues and other forms of electronic marketplaces continuously offering a variety of goods and services, making a direct connection between the technologies of TV, telephone, and computerized credit services. While regarded as the electronic equivalent of junk mail, these services are pioneering a key frontier of compunications—direct feedback, two-way communication, and the beginning of an information network.

With the use of 900-numbers, which allow for direct viewer response to questions, issues, and opinion polls, network TV has also begun to experiment with direct feedback. As with many other aspects of the compunication revolution, it is not that this is so entirely new — it is not. CUBE, the wired viewer feedback experiment in Columbus, Ohio, began in the early 1980s. Rather, it is that the capacity of this system is so great — offering much higher speed, lower cost, and greater use than the traditional systems. As powerful as the compunication revolution has been, direct feedback portends a great acceleration in the pace and expansion of its impact.

For example, since the advent of computerized credit card systems, catalogue companies have been able to reach markets with electronic sales. At the same time, TV advertisers could monitor customer response by tracking sales in a broadcast area. Both marketing techniques created feedback mechanisms that, however well tracked, had long delays built-in: catalogues have long preparation, printing, and distribution lead times; TV ads require the viewer to travel to a retail outlet. Because of the weekly shopping cycle for food and longer cycles for other goods, market trends have a minimum cycle time of weeks, at best.

New and emerging computer technologies promise to shrink this cycle time to zero. Laser-scanned uniform price codes require that a complete shopping list be put into the computer. When a customer uses a check-cashing ID card, the retailer now knows who bought what. Already, many supermarkets print real-time coupons based on purchases as a shopper goes through the checkout line: if the customer buys brand X, the checkout computer prints a coupon for brand Y. However, the potential for much more highly direct marketing is obvious.

Another dramatic use of information technology has been developed by General Motors. GM has demonstrated a computer terminal that takes a potential buyer through the entire car-buying decision with interactive software. At the end, the car dealer types in a code that sends the order directly to the factory computer, which then responds with the date and time the car will be assembled and shipped. The information is not seen or handled by another human — all the traditional information processing of middle management is accomplished automatically.

As with traditional market trends, opinion polls and voter preferences cannot be measured in very brief periods by the older methods. However, today with sophisticated electronic sampling techniques, 900-numbers, and similar feedback loops, rapid measures of public opinion and preferences can be obtained. The use of these by the major networks to be the first to call the winner of the presidential debates generates perhaps more controversy over the small sample sizes, selection process, representation criteria, and other methodological issues, as well as interpretations of the results, than it produces any clear meaning.

These are, however, issues and limitations that current and future feedback technology will quickly resolve. We will then be faced with the question of whether such rapid feedback information adds anything of value to our electoral and commercial processes. Very quickly the feedback generated by a signal, message, or process may be of much greater importance than it is — the feedback, not the medium, will be the message.

These technological variations on the existing information infrastructure are but sideshows to the emerging merger of the personal computer technology with EDIs — electronic data interchanges. Whatever technology a viewer uses for information and entertainment, he or she is still accessing a broadcast product. This infrastructure is based on information-supply push — a single product is sent to a broad audience, everybody gets the same thing.

The home PC allows a highly selective demand pull — as the viewer leaves the passive mode and becomes the active selector of the information presented. The growth of this market has been incredible — with sales of modems (including those in PCs) going from 180,000 units in 1981 to more than 8 million in 1987. Accessing a variety of information resources, data bases, networks, and EDI services, the information user identifies and selects only the information desired. This can be a consumer report on competitive products to guide a purchase choice or a review of candidates' voting records or positions to guide an election choice. It can also be a form of education and entertainment, much as one might browse in a library, an atlas, or encyclopedia. The easier the information is to access — the hardware access barriers baud, parity, and the like are no longer issues, but the software barriers still are — the greater the growth of this demand-pull infostructure will be. The great kicker in this area will be the voice-activated computer with natural language programming. Ordinary oral instructions will retrieve the desired information.

While technology has decentralized the traditional information industry, economic forces have been concentrating ownership in ever fewer hands. According to Nicholas Nichols, president of Time, Inc., soon "there will emerge, on a world wide basis, six, seven, eight vertically integrated media and entertainment mega-companies. At least one will be Japanese, probably two. We think two will be European. We think there will be a couple of American-led enterprises, and we think Time, Inc., is going to be one of them."[2] It is not much of an expansion of Mr. Nichols's definition of media and entertainment to include generic data-and-information services.

The new information technologies have given rise to whole new industries in information wholesaling and retailing. Enterprising editors have for years published various competing government handbooks based almost exclusively on the *Directory to the Federal Government,* prepared by the government at taxpayer expense and available at nominal cost through the Government Printing Office. Similar congressional directories are available. More recently, though, purveyors of innovative software buy government data wholesale (primarily from Bureau of Labor Statistics and Census Bureau) and retail them with their own analysis and access software. This is of great importance to corporations working under contract to the government, which must meet a wide array of employment and equal-opportunity standards. One package, costing more than $500,000, enables a corporation to match its employee profiles with those of the resident populations where their facilities are located, tracking on a continuous basis all major criteria of its employees and the resident labor pool on a site-by-site basis.

EXCESS CAPACITY

The models of the public issues process outlined above are based on a paradigm of looking at each issue in isolation, of one issue after another following a path like lone cars on a country road. Today, the process is more like a ten-lane interstate at rush hour, so congested that when an issue gets on, it sits in a gridlock. The fate of an issue is no longer determined by characteristics of the issue itself but by the flow (or absence of flow) of neighboring issues.

There are two forces responsible for this. First, more and more issues continue to be added to the national, state, and local agendas through the issues media—issues are backed up on the entrance ramps, waiting to start the issues process. Second, almost nothing ever leaves the agenda—there are no exit ramps.

Though some issues change priority—energy was once high—only Vietnam and Watergate have left the agenda since TV-driven issues first appeared. For those few that do leave, the coalitions behind them must execute a "March-of-Dimes" maneuver (with polio cured, the March of Dimes redefined itself to focus on birth defects). After Vietnam, the antiwar movement refocused on the environment, on peace, on legalized pot, on human, women's, gay, consumer, and animal rights movements. Lois Gibbs, a mother from Love Canal, was so successful in pushing hazardous wastes onto the national agenda that she recycled herself—she left her family to set up a consulting business.

Meanwhile, existing issues keep dividing and multiplying. The environmental issue became air, water, land, and noise pollution issues, solid wastes, recycling, underground water, hazardous materials, nuclear wastes, zero population growth, wildlife, wetlands, whales, desertification, greenhouse effect, and on and on. The clean air issue then became auto pollution, sulphur oxides, ambient air quality, indoor air quality, acid rain, and so on. When ozone and radon came along, there was no room on the national agenda.

Since each issue fragment is supported by at least one group, every issue is held as top priority by some unofficial protector of a piece of the public issues turf. Since their issue is too important for any compromise, each group must achieve total victory. No relative priorities can be set—and the issue resolution process stagnates.

But issues continue to burst upon the scene as the issues media evolve towards a more blatant advocacy role, not of any particular political orientation. The advocacy is of new issues themselves, a process of continuously searching for, promoting, exaggerating, and stimulating more and more issues. We have forgotten Will Rogers's quip, "There is not always front page news, but there is always a front page."

The relatively quiet 1980s led to a serious problem: the media that grew in capacity and technology to cover the 1960s and 1970s simply did not have enough material in the 1980s. The evening local and national news grew from 30 minutes to two and one half hours—a 500 percent increase. On cable, CNN is continuous. From the original weekly half-hour issues programs, Lawrence Spivak's *Meet the Press* and Edward R. Murrow's *See It Now,* we now have more programs daily and "specials" every week.

To fill the void, news broadcasts became "news and information shows." With the growing number, length, and commercial importance of news shows, the major networks formally mixed news and entertainment, creating infotainment. Also, issue shows, talk TV, docudrama, and assorted crime reenactment shows were born. While *60 Minutes* and similar shows explored the limits of "ambush journalism" and other sensationalisms, "tabloid TV" carved a niche for itself. As long as some people stop to gawk at the carnage of car accidents, there will be a market for pandering reporters, ever more outrageous "Geraldos"—however base.

Issues are the products of the infotainment industry. They are "sold" in ever more aggressive, attractive packages by their producers—the media.

THE SEARCH FOR NEWS: PERCEPTUAL SCOOPS

While the raw material for news programs became scarce, the competition grew as the industry decentralized. In 1970, fewer than 2 percent of U.S. homes had cable, by 1990 almost 60 percent did, with many more channels. During the 1980s, VCRs reached 70 percent of homes. The result is a vast decentralization of the media—even if ownership is more concentrated. This has heightened competition—the race to find a new issue first. In the frantic rush, many errors and mistakes are made.

Investigative reporting à la Watergate has led the search for issues to make into news. If investigative reporting had not already been invented, the pressing need to find new issues would make it necessary. All these incentives—personal, professional, and institutional—promote and reward those who uncover and hype issues. There are, after all, no rules on the admissibility of evidence in the court of public opinion.

Another impact of growth in telecommunications technologies is the disappearance of scoops. Whatever one reporter finds, virtually all other reporters can or will quickly also find. Factual scoops have become more and more rare. Of course, individuals having access to or controlling particular news stories can selectively leak them to sympathetic members of the press. Leaks are, however, different from scoops in that other reporters are blocked from the story.

Reporters still achieve a kind of scoop based on inference and perception. These scoops are subjective, based on opinion and beliefs.[3] They also lead reporters into the quicksand of news analysis. They necessarily reflect the biases and prejudices of the individual. Still, when "group-think" settles over the media and a herd mentality takes control, a single member of the press can distinguish himself or herself only by achieving an inferential or perceptual breakthrough. As there is less new in a news story, the analysis becomes a substitute for news—hard or soft. This trend is likely to continue to grow.

The rush to be first, the hype, and the other advertising tricks used to market an issue all highlight a key vulnerability of the media: the absence of checks and balances. With the blind obedience to the right to a free press, from ambush journalism to guts and gore, driven only by the ratings and commercial interests, the media are becoming a grotesque parody of the function their special freedoms are designed to promote: the creation of an informed electorate able to meet the responsibilities of a free, democratic, self-governing people, their society and government.

While the media remind us that criticisms and exposes of other institutions are "good for all," they fail to take their own medicine. Like all functions in a free society, the media need balancing mechanisms to remain healthy.

Since all national issues must necessarily involve the media, they become major players in all public debates about their role, excesses, and abuses. Even the most elementary sense of ethics should at least signal an awareness of the conflict of interests the media face; yet the conflict is not acknowledged, it is frequently denied. The media address some of their internal issues in their professional journals and societies, but all major institutions have similar self-policing functions. Moreover, the media themselves, in bypassing the internal bodies of other institutions, proclaim the necessity for an independent, external policing function—but permit none for themselves. The current debate over whether journalists, like politicians, should be required to disclose income from speaking before the groups about which they report is only the tip of the iceberg. "None-of-your-business" responses are popular—from George Will, Sam Donaldson, or James Kilpatrick—but reinforce the public perception that the press sees itself as above the standards others must meet.

In protecting their power, the media paint all critics as uneducated, uninformed cranks, nuts, and latter-day Atilla the Huns infected with a Gestapo mentality, who would repeal the First Amendment and impose the harsh censorship of a dictatorship patrolled by thought police. Such abuses of power—the stifling of public debate—are a vulnerability, the very reason that we have the special protections afforded the press: suppression of open, fair, informed public debate *by any institution* only feeds distrust, suspicion, and eventual destruction of that institution.

According to a 1988 survey by the Times Mirror Syndicate, 48 percent think press reports are "often inaccurate"—an increase of almost 50 percent since 1985. In addition, 59 percent think the press "tends to favor one side" when reporting on political and social issues, while only 18 percent rate network TV news "very favorably"—a decrease of 25 percent in two years.

By stifling debate about their excesses and abuses, the media stumble blindly into the future, unresponsive to growing suspicion and distrust. Such is the recipe for the destruction of the media as a valuable, contributing institution so vital to a free society. While the media—the Fourth Estate—want the power of an equal (if not more than equal) branch of the government, it also wants immunity from the checks and balances that operate on all other branches. Clearly, this cannot be sustained for long.

As the issues agenda reaches gridlock, the ability of the media to push yet another issue will be limited by the public's acceptance of them as an institution. The declining public acceptance of the media can be reversed only by a thorough, open, and rigorous debate on their role and their methods, abuses, and excesses.

11

The Future of the Issues Process

SYMBOLIC ISSUES

The result of the hyperactivity of the media in pushing issues onto the public agenda is shown in the 1988 presidential campaign. Critics of the 1988 U.S. presidential election decried the absence of issues, bashing both candidates for poor campaigns that lacked issues. The critics were misdirected in two ways: first, it is the response of the voters that makes an issue; and second, there were ample issues, but they were implicit, symbolic issues rather than explicit, objective issues.

Both candidates had many issue papers and offered a variety of specific proposals, but no great issues emerged to define the 1988 election. To be more specific, the differences between the candidates on these explicit issues were not sufficient to stimulate broad followings among the voters. It is not the candidates who make an issue but groups of voters who want different outcomes so much that they are willing to struggle for the support of the undecided or uninvolved voters. In neither candidate did the public find an issue with goals sufficiently different to inspire and sustain a struggle among anything close to a majority of their own supporters, much less most Americans. The candidates were neither inarticulate nor unable to communicate — there just were no fiery reactions. What did the critics want — demagogues inflaming passions over false issues?

Lacking these hard, explicit issues, the candidates — and the voters — were left with implicit, symbolic issues. Here, the candidates did have the ability to define some issues. Bush used a variety of symbols to make an issue out of Dukakis's liberalism. He linked these messages to explicit issues on which he, Dukakis, and most voters had no fighting differences — crime and defense. Who was for crime? Who was against defense? Dukakis continued to quibble about explicit issues uninteresting to most Americans and cried foul about Bush's use of the symbolic issues. He never demonstrated any understanding of symbolic issues; and in this election, the symbolic issues were stronger.

On the hard, explicit issues, voters look for a candidate who agrees with their position. In this Jacksonian style, a victory is built by adding together all the tiny fractions of a percent of the voters who agree with the candidate's position on one or more "votable" issues—Social Security, hand guns, SDI, abortion, acid rain, free trade, arms control, busing, Nicaragua, and so on.

This produces mandates. It appeals to a sense of precision—it is clear, clean, accountable—or so the critics say. It also enhances the power of political action committees—PACs and single-issue groups. And it produces the Jacksonian straightjackets that turn our political leaders into blind, robotic vote-tallying machines.

On the implicit symbolic issues, voters look for something more subtle and complex. While it would be presumptuous to stretch this to Jeffersonian democracy, it at least does move in that direction. Fundamentally, this is a process of identifying a core set of values that will be defined, protected, and promoted by the candidate's success. This involves not only what the candidate says and does but who he is—not just the personal values he will bring to future decisions but the societal values that will be recognized and rewarded by his election success.

Better and better communications technologies have changed the relationship between explicit and symbolic issues. In an election where symbolic issues dominate, the power of visual images is enhanced, matching or exceeding even those of the Nixon–Kennedy contest. Body language, eye blinks, 5-o'clock shadows, smiles, eye contact, and other nonverbal communications take on larger roles. The media may make these communications possible, but the lack of explicit issues let them dominate.

The power of subjective judgments on symbolic issues was seen as a threat to society's cherished values of objectivity and fairness. Washington insiders in particular did not like subjective judgments and symbolic issues because their influence was reduced. Hence, the once prestigious "advisors" became manipulative "handlers" and "spin doctors." If the critics had more faith in the American people, they would not have been so unhappy with this election—and they would see virtue in a more Jeffersonian process. After all, symbolic issues dominated the 1980s—explaining why people supported Reagan though they disagreed with him on most of the explicit issues. Maybe what people liked most about Reagan was the absence of fiery issues.

On the level of symbolic issues, a candidate must convince the voters that their values, beliefs, hard work, and sacrifices will be affirmed in the success of the candidate. The election became a referendum on what are America's values, with the candidates themselves as symbols. By becoming a living symbol of these values, each candidate had to assert, defend, and project his view of what these values are—or should be. This was once a tall order for a Catholic, for a divorcée, for a Southerner, for an actor—and still is for a black or a woman, among others.

The success of either Bush or Dukakis would have been a powerful affirmation of core American values—family, education, hard work, public service, integrity, the guts to overcome personal and public loss. Bush expanded his definition of America's values by both defending his values and attacking Dukakis's. By not answering attacks on liberalism, a good tactic on some explicit issues, Dukakis failed to define and defend liberal values—his values, the values millions of Americans proudly supported in the past and still honored in 1988.

His silence left *liberal* defined not from a historical perspective but as a threat to the future too horrible to be discussed in polite company. Worse, by not defending his values, Dukakis abandoned a well-established, honorable tradition and the Americans who supported it. By not defending his values, he seemed to abandon his principles. If anything was out of the mainstream of American values, this was.

The flooded national issues agenda means that there will be little room for any new issues of the traditional explicit type. Changing information technologies will continue to prod the media to advocate the candidacy of more and more issues for places on the national issues agenda. While on the one hand any issue of potential importance to the IRS may be the subject of extensive media development and coverage, there is little chance for any of the various formal authorized issue forums to address any new issue in the foreseeable future.

The important caveat is the symbolic issue—an issue that permits the public to express its frustration on a variety of not necessarily related issues, trends, institutions, and processes. The congressional pay hike, for example, amounts to less than $10 per citizen; but as a symbol of congressional arrogance, waste, greed, and irresponsibility, it was explosive. Meanwhile, the $500 billion S&L crisis, worth $2000 per citizen, stirred little public interest. The issues process need not be rational.

The secret to surviving the issues process lies in being strong enough to withstand the heat of ever greater media attention for shorter and shorter periods without panic. The media will go on to other things long before traditional institutions can begin to respond, leaving all to wonder what the fuss was about.

ISSUES MANAGEMENT

The processes of issues management continues to grow and evolve. With the shift away from the automatic legislative and regulatory response in the government arena to more anticipatory action in the private sector, the emphasis of issues management has moved from externally driven reactions to new laws and regulations, to strategies of internally focused proaction for the organization. Some observers believe the role of issues management has diminished—though CEOs now report that the time spent on external issues has grown to 70 percent.[1] Indeed, although high-visibility crisis management has diminished, the role and importance—and success—of issues management have not. Issues management is following the ancient adage of Lao Tzu: A leader leads best when in the end, the people say, "We did it ourselves!"

The concepts, principles, and processes of issues management continue to evolve, expand, and improve. Core concepts are being recognized and established. The Edison Electric Institute recently released a report validating three issues management process models, including the one presented above.[2] At major universities, courses on issues management are growing, as are centers for the application and research of issues management concepts. The frontier is active, with creative minds exploring a wide variety of concepts and applications of issues management.

The major impact of issues management is only now being felt. It remains to be seen whether IM's role in privatizing the public issue process is a step forward, whether the frustration of the Washington issue activists can ignite a grassroots backfire, whether the Congress—or any public leader or group—will care that the Congress is being cut out of the policy-making loop.

The old process is fading, and a new one is not yet well established. This is changing the balance of power among strong, well-organized, capable adversarial groups and institutions. It is not likely to be done quietly.

Conclusion

IN SEARCH OF CORPORATE STATESMANSHIP

As CEOs assume roles traditionally held by politicians, they are finding that many of the rules politicians observe apply, though there are no campaigns, no elections, no hearings to hold, no votes to cast, no constituents to help—at least not in the CEO's job description. Nevertheless, the rules are still there.

A politician learns that others have ideas for "new" issues—some so long ago, the newness has long worn off. In the U.S. Congress, rare is the new issue that some member has not already seen and addressed. At a very minimum, members learn that their issues research must find, identify, analyze, and distinguish the positions of others who came before them. Once they have spoken, their words can never be changed.

A second key rule politicians learn to observe is that of *standing*—they must have standing to address an issue. A congressman from New York City does not touch a farm issue. Should he find himself on the Agricultural Committee, he can address farm issues only as an Agricultural Committee member. This is not just professional courtesy, it is a public necessity. Presidential candidate Al Gore hurt himself badly in 1988 when without any standing he took on a major arms control issue. He had a good idea, and the more press he got, the worse his criticism got. Finally, he was denounced by leaders in his own party and saw his influence in the House decline. He has not repeated the error as a senator.

In the private sector, standing can be established in a variety of ways. Lee Iacocca has standing to address U.S. trade relations with Japan because he made a public mission to restore quality—part of the root problem of U.S.

competition with Japan. Ford's CEO has done just as much privately, but even if Petersen said the same words as Iacocca, all he would hear is, "Who?" GE's Jack Welch has tried to follow Reginald Jones's example, but by addressing too broad a spectrum of issues too quickly, he lost his standing; and all he heard was speculation about his Senate ambitions.

Illiteracy is an issue of great concern in the United States. Many corporate CEOs have addressed the issue, most notably AMOCO's Richard Morrow, Sears's Edward Brennan, Bell South's John Clendenin. All have some standing. But two have achieved special standing, though quite differently: AT&T's vice chairman Charles Marshall has focused on New York City—AT&T makes its corporate home there and is a consumer of NYC's educational product; Xerox's David Kearns knows that every college graduate in America has used Xerox's educational products. Xerox supplies educational products because Xerox believes in education. Marshall and Kearns have standing on education issues.

The requirement of standing forces a sobering dose of reality and urges humility. Donald Trump, a wealthy young New York developer, learned the hard way when he ignored all his local options and New York's abundant list of pressing issues to address the general public on the role of military force in U.S. foreign policy, spending half a million dollars to publish his ideas in all the major newspapers. Even among those who agreed with his every word, he was seen as a novice, unstable, a pushy loudmouth who has more money than sense. Of all possible subjects, foreign policy is the most sensitive to and least tolerant of such surprise stunts. His message was quickly swamped by stories of its costs and speculation about his real purpose. If he had built some standing—and he could have—he might have been heard. As a developer, he does have standing to address a host of urban issues—congestion, pollution, waste management, affordable housing, property taxes, crime, the homeless, and the like.

In America today, if a CEO has too little standing for the issues he seeks to address, the presumption is that he has made plans to leave his post but does not yet know where he is going. Increasingly, this works against both his and the corporation's best interests.

For this reason, America's corporate statesmen limit their personal participation to issues where they and their corporations have clear standing as seen by the audience they address. Where CEOs seek to address issues with less standing, they focus on the specific publics where their standing is greatest. Trump could have started with a speech at New York's Foreign Policy Council and offered it to the *New York Times* to reprint as a guest column. Eventually, through careful positioning over time, a CEO can build standing in a new area.

Like the politician, the CEO must have good issues research, the best forecasts of current and future trends, and thoroughly survey the setting before moving into it with careful assessments of ever changing public opinion. Politicians call it "good staffing"; and they don't last long without it. As the private sector plays a growing role in the public issues process, CEOs are using issues management concepts and methods to meet the challenge of their changing roles.

The coauthor of *The Public Affairs Handbook* (with William L. Renfro among others), Arco's chairman, Robert Anderson, described the new working environment of American business:

Failure to perform competently and credibly in the realm of public issues can be devastating to the prospects of any business. It is not stretching fact at all to say that business today has a new bottom line—public acceptance. Without the approval and support of society, it's obvious that financial success is irrelevant.

Anderson sounds more like a radical anticapitalist than a leading corporate statesman. Yet, the power of his observation is clear: Greece saw a major industry—tourism—collapse when it bungled the issue of airport security; Audi lost 85 percent of its American car market when it mishandled the "sudden-acceleration" issue; Perrier's confused response over benzene showed, in fact, that Perrier is not perfect but has to be processed like all other water. None of these will ever regain with this generation of American consumers the public acceptance it once had.

It is the grudging realization of the validity of Anderson's observation that drives the issues management process in America's largest corporations. His words are the preamble of the new private sector Constitution, the radical new social contract being written by and for American business. In the dynamic world of public issues, CEOs and their corporations must continue to reinvent themselves, anticipating and adapting to the rapidly changing rules of the public issue process—by which they prosper or perish.

Notes

CHAPTER 1

1. The twentieth-century management literature is replete with admonitions to look forward, perhaps because our culture is built up from the individual experience where the rowing perspective — divining the path ahead by viewing the past — prevails. Kierkegaard sums up the traditional orientation: Life must be lived forwards, but it can only be understood backwards. However, what may work for the individual may not be best for the group — especially when the mission of the group is not understanding life but achieving some specific accomplishments. From conversations with the Rev. John Harper, St. John's Episcopal Church, LaFayette Square, Washington, D.C. 1991.

2. National Highway Safety Administration data.

3. President Truman appointed the Materials Policy Commission with CBS's William Paley as chairman in 1951.

4. In Greek mythology, the prophetess Cassandra was cursed by Apollo to give accurate prophecies that would never be believed.

5. In *Issue Management: Origin of the Future,* W. Howard Chase presents issue action plans as a step of the issues management process.

6. Unable to bring the Federal Trade Commission under control by anything short of new legislation, Congress eliminated the FTC budget several times in the early 1980s.

7. Since the *Roe* v. *Wade* decision in 1973, both sides have taken the abortion issue to every national issues resolution forum — the Congress, the states, regulatory agencies, the White House — without resolution.

8. Fernand Braudel, *The Mediterranean and the Mediterranean World in the Age of Phillip II* (London: Collins, 1972).

9. William Manchester, *The Glory and The Dream* (New York: Random House, 1974).

10. The White House Conference on Global Change, Washington, D.C. April 1990.

11. Sir Alfred North Whitehead, 1931.

12. Alvin Toffler, *Future Shock* (New York: Random House, 1970).

13. The Club of Rome, The Limits to Growth: A Report for the Club of Rome's Project on the Predicament of Mankind (New York: Universal Books, 1972).

14. Probabilistic System Dynamics (PSD) was conceptualized by Ted Gordon in 1974. Mihael Mesarovich perfected a series of PSD models over the last eighteen years.

15. William L. Renfro, "Policy Impact Analysis: A Step beyond Forecasting," *World Future Society Journal,* September 1980.

16. H. G. Wells, *The Discovery of the Future,* July 1903, reprinted in the *Futures Research Quarterly,* Winter 1985.

17. Joseph Nagelschmidt, ed., *The Public Affairs Handbook* (New York: AMACOM, 1982).

CHAPTER 2

1. Fred Pauls, "Social Protection Legislation of the Congress," *Fred Pauls, Congressional Research Service,* Report 79-382, July 1979.

2. "Pain Still Burns at Happyland a Year Later," *Washington Post,* April 8, 1991.

3. Robert O. Anderson, Preface, in *The Public Affairs Handbook,* ed. Joe Nagleschmidt (New York: AMACOM, 1982).

4. Allen Schick, *Manual on the Federal Budget Process* (Washington, D.C.: Congressional Research Service, Report #87-286, March 31, 1987).

5. The Foresight Provision (Rules of the House of Representatives, [cl. 2 (b)(1), Rule X], Jefferson's Manual, sec., 692[a], 102nd Congress, 1993).

6. Barbara Reynolds, *USA Today,* interview of Eddie Fraser, February 13, 1987.

7. Congressmen Cochran, Dingell, and Gore formed the Congressional Foresight Network on September 2, 1982.

8. The Congressional Research Service formed the Futures Research Group as part of the Science Policy Division shortly after the House foresight rule was adopted in 1974.

9. The life cycle of public issues was based on the traditional product life cycle model. See any standard text.

10. The life cycle of public issues was presented to the public in Toronto, in August 1980, at the World Futures Society meeting. See also William Renfro, "Forecasting the US Legislative Environment," SRI International's Business Intelligence Program, Report 644, December 1980; idem., "Managing the Issues of the 1980s," *The Futurist* (World Futures Society) March 1982; idem., "Issues Management," *Futures,* (London, August 1988).

11. "Love Canal Revisited," *Washington Post,* April 18, 1986.

12. Ombudsman, *Washington Post,* Op-Ed page, December 2, 1990.

13. "The End of the Thatcher Era," *London Times,* November 24, 1990.

14. Mark Anderson, "Balloon Industry Struggles to Rise above the Barbs," *Wall Street Journal,* June 27, 1991.

15. Trish Hall, "How Classroom Crusaders Saved the Dolphin from the Net," *New York Times,* April 18, 1990.

16. Frank Cerabino, "'Ladies' Adopt Dog-Write-Dog Lobbying Tactic," *Palm Beach Post,* April 24, 1992.

17. James E. Lukaszewski, "Managing Fear," *Vital Speeches,* February 1, 1992, p. 238; "It Ain't Easy Being Green," idem., June 15, 1991, p. 532; "Managing Bad News in America," idem., July 1, 1990, p. 568; *Influencing Public Attitudes* (Leesburg, Va: Issue Action Publications, 1992).

18. William Renfro, "Business Government Relations: A New Paradigm," speech to the Public Issues Forum of the Brookings Institution, July 15, 1987.

19. "101st Congress Churns toward Adjournment," *Washington Post,* October 27, 1990.

20. H. Jane Lehman, "Housing Law Spurs Anger in Retirement Communities," *Washington Post,* March 31, 1987. The new legislation was first enforced in 1989 in a suit brought by the Department of Justice. See Gwen Ifill, "U.S. Sues over Adults-Only Rentals," *Washington Post,* April 19, 1989.

21. Terminating Programs File, SCORPIO Congressional Computerized Information System, annual data.

22. Gerald Edgly, Project Director, *Models for Issues Management,* prepared by J. F. Coates (Washington, D.C.: Edison Electric Institute, 1986). As used herein, the models studied in the EEI report are models of the public issues process, not issues management. A model for the internal organizational process called issues management is presented in Chapter 9.

23. Doug Henton, Tom Chmura, and William Renfro, *State Government Issues for Business* (Menlo Park, Calif.: SRI International, Business Intelligence Program, No. 711, Fall 1984).

24. Council of State Governments, Iron Works Pike, Lexington, Kentucky.

25. William Renfro, "The 100th Congress: A Lame Duck Legislature," *Vital Speeches of the Day* 54 (3): 95.

26. David Broder, "How about a Little Glasnost for the House," *Washington Post,* May 29, 1989; "The Need For House Repair," *New York Times,* July 9, 1988.

27. See college or advanced physics texts such as David Halliday and Robert Resnick, *Fundamentals of Physics* (New York: John Wiley & Son, 1988); Robert Eisenberg and Robert Resnick, *Quantum Physics of Atoms, Molecules, Solids, Nuclei and Particles* (New York: John Wiley & Son, 1974); or A. Kaplan, *Nuclear Physics* (New York: John Wiley, 1965).

CHAPTER 3

1. Peter Drucker, *Management* (New York: Random House, 1972).

2. William Renfro, "Forecasting Public Policies," *Long Range Planning,* August, 1980.

CHAPTER 4

1. W. Howard Chase, *Issue Management: Origin of the Future* (Leesburg, Va: Issue Action Publications, 1985). See also *The Chase-Jones Issue Management Model* (Leesburg, Va: Issue Action Publications, 1979).

CHAPTER 5

1. *Models for Issues Management,* Edison Electric Institute, see Chapter 2, note 22.
2. Joseph Aguilar, *Business Scanning* (Cambridge: Harvard University Press, 1965).
3. Hank Koehn, Vice President, Security Pacific National Bank, meeting of the American Bankers Association, May 1989.
4. For descriptions of NGT and the Delphi method, see any standard text.
5. William Renfro, "Future Histories: A New Scenario Technique," *The Futurist,* August 1989.
6. General Charles W. Bagnal, project leader, "The Professional Development of Officers Study" (Washington, D.C.: Department of the Army, Office of the Chief of Staff, Fall 1985).

CHAPTER 6

1. Part of this discussion appeared in "Issues Management: The American Experience," *The Journal of the International Public Relations Association,* Fall 1990.
2. World Future Society Conference, August 1986, New York, N.Y., panel discussion on "My Favorite Scanning Resources and Methods," chaired by W. Renfro, available on tape from WFS, Bethesda, MD.
3. *FutureScan* is published weekly by Dr. Roger Silbert, Los Angeles, CA, at a nominal cost. *Corporate Public Issues,* founded by Howard Chase, is published by Issue Action Publications of Leesburg, VA. *FutureSurvey* is published by the World Futures Society, Bethesda, MD. *The Issues Management Association Newsletter* is published by IMA, Washington, D.C.
4. Brook Tunstall, *Disconnecting Parties: The Break-up of AT&T* (Princeton: Princeton University Press, 1987). Charles Brown, working with Jim Armstrong, drafted a chapter for the 1982 *Public Affairs Handbook* on AT&T's issues management program that handled the breakup. However, when the breakup was delayed at the last moment, he withdrew the chapter.
5. AT&T Corporate Planning Emerging Issues Group, Emily R. Coleman, Project Director, *The Context of Legislation* (Basking Ridge, N.J.: March 1980).

CHAPTER 7

1. Niccolò di Bernardo Machiavelli, *The Prince.*
2. John Gall, *Systemantics: How Systems Work and Especially How They Fail* (New York: Quadrangle/NYT Book Co., 1977).
3. See any modern text on organizational development.
4. Though it is popular to decry change, Americans thrive on it. The real meaning of complaints about change seems to be that Americans do not like to be the implements of change but rather the implementators of change—the changer, not the changed.
5. The core concepts of this section, presented at the World Futures Society Conference, Washington, D.C., August 1988, appeared in *Vanguard,* a foresight publication of the American Society of Association Executives, December 1988.

6. Based on an article published by the Issues Management Association in its newsletter, September 1986.

7. Winslow's Law was postulated in the 1980s by Dr. Eric Winslow, dean of management science, School of Government and Business Administration, the George Washington University Graduate School, Washington, D.C.

CHAPTER 9

1. Lloyd Grove, "The Angel of Cartoon Heaven," *Washington Post,* May 14, 1986.

2. *New York Times,* May 5, 1991.

3. "Meese fires spokesman over cartoon what's your sign — 'For Sale' in Kansas City Star," Terry Eastland, *New York Times,* May 17, 1988.

4. "Network Joke Barometer the role of Johnny Carson," *Washington Post,* March 26, 1989.

CHAPTER 10

1. Information Industries Association, Washington, D.C.

2. *Washington Post,* April 9, 1989.

3. *Washington Post Magazine,* October 7, 1990.

CHAPTER 11

1. Barbara Reynolds, *USA Today,* interview of Eddie Fraser, February 13, 1987.

2. *Models for Issues Management,* Edison Electric Institute.

Appendixes

Appendix

A

Scanning Resources

The following publications are popularly used in U.S. scanning systems. They must be supplemented by similar resources from other media—radio, television, conferences, forums, hearings. For a discussion, see "Scanning" in Chapter 5.

Figure A.1
Popular National Scanning Resources

AMERICAN HEALTH		NEW AGE	
	HEALTH		HIGH TECH
ATTENZIONE		NEW BODY	
	HEAVY METAL		SAVVY
BARTER NEWS		NEW REPUBLIC	
	HORIZON		SCIENCE DIGEST
BLACK COLLEGIAN		NUTRITION HEALTH	
	INC.		SEVENTEEN
BUSINESS WEEK		ODYSSEY	
	JET		TECHNOLOGY ILLUSTRATED
CAMPUS LIFE		OMNI	
	LADIES HOME JOURNAL		US
CATHOLIC DIGEST		PARENTS	
	LEARNING REVIEW		VEGETARIAN TIMES
COLUMBIA JOURNAL		PEOPLE	
	MEDICAL UPDATE		VENTURE
COMPUTERS & ELECTRONICS		PERSONAL COMPUTING	
	MEDICAL HOTLINE		VILLAGE VOICE
CONSUMERS DIGEST		VANITY FAIR	
	MOTHER EARTH NEWS		WORKING MOTHER
DISCOVER		PREVENTION	
	MONEY		WORLD PRESS REVIEW
EAST WEST JOURNAL		PSYCHOLOGY TODAY	
	MOTHER JONES		LA FREE PRESS
EBONY		READERS DIGEST	
	MS		WORLD VIEW
HARPERS		ROLLING STONE	
	NATIONAL LAMPOON		YOUNG MS

The following publications are part of the scanning network operated by the American Council of Life Insurance, Washington, D.C.

Across the Board
Administrative Management
Advertising Age
Aging
Aging & Work
American Banker
American Bar Association Journal
American Demographics
American Medical News
American Scholar
American Scientist
Architectural Record
Atlantic Monthly

Behavior Today
Brain Mind Bulletin
Brookings Review
Bulletin of Atomic Scientists
Business and Society Review
Business Horizons
The Business Quarterly
Business Week

California Management Review
Canadian Business & Science
Center Magazine
Change—Magazine of Higher Education
Channels
Chronicle of Higher Education
Christian Science Monitor
CoEvolution Quarterly
Columbia Journalism Review

Daedalus
Datamation
Discover
Dun's Business Monthly

East West Journal
The Economist
Emerging Trends

Family Planning Perspectives
Financial Planner
Financial Times
Footnotes to the Future
Forbes
Foreign Affairs
Free Lance

Futures
Future Society
The Futurist

Geo
The Gerontologist

Harpers'
Harvard Business Review
Harvard Medical Letter
Hastings Center Report
High Technology
Humanist

Industry Week
In These Times
Institute of Noetic Sciences Newsletter

Journal of Business Strategy
Journal of Communication
Journal of Consumer Affairs
Journal of Contemporary Business
Journal of Insurance
Journal of Long Range Planning
Journal of Social Issues

Leading Edge

Management World
Medical Economics
Medical World News
Money Magazine
Monthly Labor Review
Mother Jones
Ms.

New Age
Nation's Business
New England Journal of Medicine
New Republic
New Scientist
New Times
New York Review of Books
New York Times
Newsweek
Nuclear Times

Off Our Backs
Omni

Personal Computing
Personnel Journal
Policy Studies Review
The Progressive
Psychology Today
Public Opinion
Public Interest
Public Relations Journal

Quest

Rain
Resurgence
Rolling Stone

Saturday Night
Saturday Review
Savvy
Science
Science and Public Policy
Science Digest
Science News
The Science (NY Academy of Science)
Science Technology & Human Values
Scientific American
Sloan Management Review
Smithsonian

Social Policy
Society
Solar Age

Tarrytown
Technology Forecasts
Technology Illustrated
Technology Review
Time
To the Point

Urban Futures Idea Exchange
USA Today
US News & World Report

Vital Speeches of the Day

Wall Street Journal
Washington Monthly
The Warton
What's Next
The Wilson Quarterly
World Future Society Bulletin
Working Papers for New Society
Working Woman
World Press Review

B

Issues Management Periodicals

The following periodicals regularly publish articles that may be of interest to professionals involved in issues management.

Advertising Age
Association Trends
Business Quarterly
California Management Review
Corporate Public Issues
Editorial Research Reports (by Congressional Quarterly)
Future Survey
Futures
Futures Research Quarterly
The Futurist
The Gallagher Report
Harvard Business Review
International Public Relations Association Review
Issues Management Letter
The Journal of Business Strategy
Long Range Planning
Management Communication Quarterly
Perspectives (from Public Affairs Council)
Planning Review
Public Relations Journal
Public Relations Reporter
Public Relations Review
Speech Writers Newsletter
Strategic Management Journal
Vanguard (by American Society of Association Executives)
Vital Speeches
What's Next (by the Congressional Clearinghouse on the Future)

C

Professional Organizations

Many groups offer some aspects of issues management to their members and the list below is by no means complete. These organizations have issues management as their primary mission or one of their primary missions.

American Bar Association, Chicago, Ill.
American Society of Association Executives, Washington, D.C.
Business Higher Education Forum, Washington, D.C.
Business Roundtable, Washington, D.C.
The Brookings Institution, Washington, D.C.
The Conference on Issues and the Media, Alexandria, Va.
International Association of Business Communicators, Washington, D.C.
International Public Relations Association, London, U.K.
The Issue Exchange, Leesburg, Va.
Issues Management Association, Washington, D.C.
Lawyers for the Republic, Washington, D.C.
National Association of Republican Lawyers, Washington, D.C.
National Bar Association, Washington, D.C.
Public Relations Society of America, Public Affairs Section, New York, N.Y.
Public Affairs Council, Washington, D.C. The council conducted the first national issues management conference in 1976.
Risk Management Institute, New York, N.Y.
The World Futures Society, Bethesda, Md.
Women in Government Relations, Washington, D.C.

Bibliography

BOOKS

Aguilar, F. R. (1967) *Scanning the Business Environment*. New York: Macmillan.

Balderston, F. E., J. M. Carman, and F. M. Nicosia, eds. (1981) *Regulation of Marketing and the Public Interest*. New York: Pergamon.

Barnard, C. (1938) *The Functions of the Executive*. Cambridge: Harvard University Press.

Bean, L. H. (1969) *The Art of Forecasting*. New York: Random House.

Bell, D. (1973) *The Coming of Post-Industrial Society: A Venture in Social Forecasting*. New York: Basic Books.

Benson, J. K. (1982) A Framework for Policy Analysis. In D. L. Rogel, D. A. Whetten and Associates (eds.) *Interorganizational Coordination: Theory, Research and Implementation*. Ames, Iowa: Iowa State University Press.

Bigelow, B., L. Fahey, and J. F. Mahon. (1991) Political Strategy and Issues Evolution: A Framework for Analysis and Action. In K. Paul (ed.) *Contemporary Issues in Business and Politics*. Lewiston, N.Y.: Edwin Mellen Press.

Boucher, W. I., ed. (1977) *The Study of the Future: An Agenda for Research*. Washington, D.C.: National Science Foundation.

Brown, A., and E. Weiner. (1984) *Supermanaging*. New York: McGraw-Hill.

Buchholz, R. A. (1985) *Essentials of Public Policy for Management*. Englewood Cliffs, N.J.: Prentice-Hall.

Buchholz, R. A., W. D. Evans, and R. O. Wagley. (1985) *Management Response to Public Issues: Concepts and Cases in Strategy Formulation*. Englewood Cliffs, N.J.: Prentice-Hall.

Carnoy, M., and D. Shearer. (1980) *Economic Democracy: The Challenge of the 1980s*. Armonk, N.Y.: M. E. Sharpe.

Chase, W. H. (1984) *Issue Management: Origins of the Future*. Stamford, Conn.: Issue Action Publications.

Chemical Manufacturers Association, ed. (1983) *Risk Management of Existing Chemicals.* Rockville, Md.: Government Institutes.

Cobb, R. W., and C. D. Elder. (1972) *Participation in American Politics: The Dynamics of Agenda Building.* Baltimore, Md.: Johns Hopkins University Press.

Coppa and Avery Consultants. (1985) *Contingency Planning and Management: A Bibliographical Guide.* Monticello, Ill.: Vance Bibliographies.

Corrado, F. M. (1984) *Media for Managers.* Englewood Cliffs, N.J.: Prentice-Hall.

DiGaetani, J. L. (1986) *The Handbook of Executive Communication.* Homewood, Ill.: Dow Jones–Irwin.

Edelman, M. (1964) *The Symbolic Uses of Politics.* Chicago, Ill.: University of Illinois Press.

Etzioni, A. (1983) *An Immodest Agenda: Rebuilding America Before the 21st Century.* New York: McGraw-Hill.

Ewing, R. P. (1987) *Managing the New Bottom Line: Issues Management for Senior Executives.* Homewood, Ill.: Dow Jones–Irwin.

Eyestone, R. (1978) *From Social Issues to Social Policy.* New York: Wiley.

Fine, S. H. (1981) *The Marketing of Ideas and Social Issues.* New York: Praeger.

Finsterbusch, K., L. G. Llewellyn, and C. P. Wolf, eds. (1983) *Social Impact Assessment Methods.* Beverly Hills, Calif.: Sage Publications.

Gollner, A. B. (1983) *Social Change and Corporate Strategy: The Expanding Role of Public Affairs.* Stamford, Conn.: Issue Action Publications.

Grefe, E. A. (1981) *Fighting to Win: Business Political Power.* New York: Harcourt Brace Jovanovich.

Hall, P. (1980) *Great Planning Disasters.* Berkeley and Los Angeles: University of California Press.

Heath, R. L., and R. A. Nelson. (1986) *Issues Management.* Beverly Hills, Calif.: Sage Publications.

Heclo, H. (1978) Issue Networks and the Executive Establishment. In A. King (ed.) *The New American Political System.* Washington, D.C.: American Enterprise Institute.

Kingdon, J. W. (1984) *Agendas, Alternatives, and Public Policies.* New York: John Wiley & Sons.

Kuhn, A. J. (1986) *Organizational Cybernetics and Business Policy: System Design for Performance Control.* University Park: Pennsylvania State University Press.

Lukaszewski, James E. (1992) *Influencing Public Attitudes.* Leesburg, Va.: Issue Action Publications.

Mendell, J., ed. (1985) *Nonextrapolative Methods in Business Forecasting.* Westport, Conn.: Quorum Press.

Morrison, J. L., W. L. Renfro, and W. I. Boucher. (1983) *Applying Methods and Techniques of Futures Research.* Washington, D.C.: Jossey-Bass.

——. (1984) *Futures Research and the Strategic Planning Process.* Washington, D.C.: ERIC Clearinghouse.

Nagelschmidt, J. S., ed. (1982) *The Public Affairs Handbook.* New York: AMACOM.

Nowlan, S. E., and D. R. Shayon. (1984) *Leveraging the Impact of Public Affairs.* Philadelphia: Human Resource Network.

Paluszek, J. L. (1977) *Will the Corporation Survive?* Reston, Va.: Reston Publishing.

Polak, F. (1973) *The Image of the Future,* trans. by E. Boulding. New York: Elsevier Scientific Publishing Company.

Post, J. E. (1978) *Corporate Behavior and Social Change.* Reston, Va.: Reston Publishing.

Preston, L., ed. (1978) *Research in Corporate Social Performance and Policy,* vol. 1. Greenwich, Conn.: JAI Press.

——. (1980) *Research in Corporate Social Performance and Policy,* vol. 2. Greenwich, Conn.: JAI Press.

——. (1981) *Research in Corporate Social Performance and Policy,* vol. 3. Greenwich, Conn.: JAI Press.

——. (1982) *Research in Corporate Social Performance and Policy,* vol. 4. Greenwich, Conn.: JAI Press.

Preston, L. E., and J. E. Post. (1975) *Private Management and Public Policy: The Principle of Public Responsibility.* Englewood Cliffs, N.J.: Prentice-Hall.

Renfro, W. L. (1982) *The Legislative Role of Corporations.* New York: AMACOM.

Schendel, D. E., and C. W. Hofer, eds. (1979) *Strategic Management: A New View of Business Policy and Planning.* Boston: Little, Brown.

Sethi, S. Prakash, and C. M. Falbe. (1987) *Business and Society: Dimensions of Conflict and Cooperation.* Lexington, Mass.: Lexington Books.

Sheppard, C. S., and D. C. Carroll, eds. (1980) *Working in the Twenty-First Century.* New York: Wiley.

Snyder, D. P., and G. Edwards. (1984) *Future Forces: An Association Executive's Guide to a Decade of Change and Choice.* Washington, D.C.: Foundation of the American Society of Association Executives.

Sowell, T. (1987) *Conflict of Visions.* New York: William Morrow.

Stanley, G. D. (1985) *Managing External Issues: Theory and Practice.* Greenwich, Conn.: JAI Press.

Starling, G., and O. W. Baskin. (1985) *Issues in Business and Society: Capitalism and Public Purpose.* Boston: Kent Publishing Company.

Tombari, H. A. (1984) *Business and Society.* New York: Dryden Press.

Tunstall, W. B. (1985) *Disconnecting Parties: Managing the Bell System Break-Up, an Inside View.* New York: McGraw-Hill.

Twiss, B. C., ed. (1982) *Social Forecasting for Company Planning.* London: Macmillan.

Vance, M. (1982) *Communication in Management.* Monticello, Ill.: Vance Bibliographies.

Warren, E. K. (1966) *Long-Range Planning: The Executive Viewpoint.* Englewood Cliffs, N.J.: Prentice-Hall.

Yankelovich, Daniel. (1981) *New Rules.* New York: Random House.

PROFESSIONAL JOURNALS

Arrington, R. A., and R. N. Sawaya. (1984, Summer) "Managing public affairs: issues management in an uncertain environment." *California Management Review,* pp. 148–160.

Banks, L. (1978, March-April) "Taking on the hostile media." *Harvard Business Review,* pp. 123–130.

Barrows, D. S., and S. Morris. (1989, December) "Managing public policy issues." *Long Range Planning* (UK), pp. 66–73.

Bartha, P. F. (1982, Autumn) "Managing corporate external issues: an analytical framework." *Business Quarterly,* pp. 78–90.

Baysinger, B. D. (1984, No. 2) "Domain maintenance as an objective of business political activity: an expanded typology." *Academy of Management Review,* pp. 248–258.

Becker, H. S. (1983, May) "Scenarios: a tool of growing importance to policy analysts in government and industry." *Technological Forecasting and Social Change,* pp. 95–120.

Bergner, D. (1984, April) "Guidelines on integrating international public affairs." *Perspectives,* pp. 1–4.

——. (1982, Summer) "Political risk analysis." *Public Relations Quarterly,* pp. 28–31.

——. (1982, June) "The role of strategic planning in international public affairs." *Public Relations Journal,* pp. 32–33.

Bloom, P. N., and L. W. Stern. (1976, October) "Emergence of anti-industrialism." *Business Horizons,* pp. 87–93.

Boddewyn, J. J. (1982, Winter) "Advertising regulation in the 1980s: the underlying global forces." *Journal of Marketing,* pp. 27–35.

Boe, A. (1979, Winter) "Fitting the corporation to the future." *Public Relations Quarterly,* pp. 4–6.

Bogan, C. (1984, November) "Future U." *American Way,* pp. 71–74.

Bower, C. D., and J. J. Hallett. (1989, January) "Issues management at ASPA." *Personnel Administrator,* pp. 40–43.

Brodwin, D. R., and L. J. Bourgeois III. (1984, Spring) "Five steps to strategic action." *California Management Review,* pp. 176–190.

Buchholz, R. A. (1982, No. 3) "Education for public issues management: insights from a survey of top practitioners." *Public Affairs Review,* pp. 65–76.

Cammillus, J. C., and D. K. Datta. (1991, April) "Managing strategic issues in a turbulent environment." *Long Range Planning,* pp. 67–74.

Campbell, R. S., and L. O. Levine. (1983, April) "Patent analysis: tracking technology trends." *Battelle Today,* pp. 3–6.

Campbell, T. W. (1983, August) "Identifying the issues." *Public Relations Journal,* pp. 19–20.

"Capitalizing on social change." (1979, October 29) *Business Week,* pp. 23, 24.

Carroll, A. B., and F. Hoy. (1984) "Integrating corporate social policy into strategic management." *Journal of Business and Society,* pp. 48–57.

Cathey, P. (1982, April 23) "Industry has a new advance guard—issues managers." *Iron Age,* pp. 64–70.

Chase, W. H. (1980, Spring) "Prelude to the '80s: adjusting to a different business/ social climate." *Public Relations Quarterly,* pp. 24–26.

——. (1977, October) "Public issue management: the new science." *Public Relations Journal,* pp. 25–26.

Clark, T. B. (1986, April 19) "Divided they stand." *National Journal,* pp. 928–933.

Coates, J. F., and J. S. Feher. (1986, Fall) "A research agenda for issues management." *Futures Research Quarterly,* pp. 72–92.

Coates, J. F., and J. Jarratt. (1986, Spring) "Mapping the issues of an industry: an exercise in issues identification." *Futures Research Quarterly,* pp. 53–63.

Cook, L. (1986, Spring) "The state scanning network: an issue identification system for state policy managers." *Futures Research Quarterly,* pp. 65–77.

Crable, R. E., and S. L. Vibbert. (1985, Summer) "Managing issues and influencing public policy." *Public Relations Review,* pp. 3–16.

Dickie, R. B. (1984, No. 5) "Influence of public affairs offices on corporate planning and of corporations on government policy." *Strategic Management Journal,* pp. 15–33.

Dilenschneider, R. L. (1985, April) "Anticipation: a key weapon in crisis strategy." *IABC Communication World,* pp. 30–31.

Divilbiss, R. I., and M. R. Cullen, Jr. (1981, Spring) "Business, the media, and the American public." *MSU Business Topics,* pp. 21–28.

Ehrbar, A. F. (1978, August 28) "Backlash against business advocacy." *Fortune,* pp. 62–64.

Ellis, R. J. (1982, Winter) "Improving management response in turbulent times." *Sloan Management Review,* pp. 3–12.

Ernstthal, H. (1985, Winter) "Trade association activism: managing issues and affecting public policy." *Futures Research Quarterly,* pp. 84–93.

Evans, F. J. (1981, November–December) "Academics, the new class and antibusiness ideology." *Business Horizons,* pp. 40–47.

Ewing, R. P. (1990, Spring) "Moving from micro to macro issues management." *Public Relations Review,* pp. 19–24.

——. (1982, No. 3) "Advocacy advertising: the voice of business in public policy debate." *Public Affairs Review,* pp. 23–31.

——. (1980, June) "Evaluating issues management." *Public Relations Journal,* pp. 14–16.

——. (1976, December 6) "New corporate role: customers' advocate." *PR Reporter.*

——. (1979, Winter) "Uses of futurist techniques in issues management." *Public Relations Quarterly,* pp. 15–19.

——. (1980, December 13) "Who owns the First Amendment?" *PR/Chicago.*

Fahey, L., and W. R. King. (1977, August) "Environmental scanning for corporate planning." *Business Horizons,* pp. 61–71.

Finn, D. (1978, February) "Why business has trouble with the media, and vice versa." *Across the Board,* pp. 55–60.

"Five top issues of next five years identified in IMA's second survey." (1987, Spring) *The 'IMA' Newsletter,* p. 1.

Fleming, J. E. (1980, Winter) "Linking public affairs with corporate planning." *California Management Review,* pp. 35–43.

Fox, J. F. (1982, Summer) "Communicating on public issues." *Public Relations Quarterly,* pp. 19–26.

——. (1982, August) "The politicizing of the chief executive." *Public Relations Journal,* pp. 20–24.

"Fox supports new Issues Management Association." (1982, May 19) *Jack O'Dwyer's Newsletter,* p. 2.

Goldman, E. (1982, No. 3) "On the growing need for business to take arms against a sea of initiative troubles." *Public Affairs Review,* pp. 47–55.

Goodman, S. E. (1983, April) "Why few corporations monitor social issues." *Public Relations Journal,* p. 20.

Gottschalk, E. C., Jr. (1988) "Firms hiring new type of manager to study issues, emerging troubles." *Wall Street Journal,* June 10.

"Governors establish trend-detecting network." (1984, November 5) *Leading Edge,* pp. 1-3.

Gray, D. H. (1986, January-February) "Uses and misuses of strategic planning." *Harvard Business Review*, pp. 89-97.

Hainsworth, B., and M. Meng. (1988, Winter) "How corporations define issue management." *Public Relations Review*, pp. 18-30.

Hamermesh, R. G. (1986, July-August) "Making planning strategic." *Harvard Business Review*, pp. 115-120.

Hayes, R. H. (1985, November-December) "Strategic planning — forward in reverse?" *Harvard Business Review*, pp. 111-119.

Heath, R. L., and Cousino, K. R. (1990, Spring) "Issues management: end of first decade progress report." *Public Relations Review*, pp. 6-18.

Heenan, D. A. (1982, Winter) "Ideology revisited: America looks ahead." *Sloan Management Review*, pp. 35-46.

Hilgartner, S., and C. I. Bosk. (1988) "The rise and fall of social problems: a public arenas model." *American Journal of Sociology*, pp. 53-78.

Hing, A. (1990, Summer) "Issues management and influencing decisions." *Practicing Manager* (Australia), pp. 42-44.

"How fast do new ideas percolate through pr ranks?" (1983, January 24) *PR Reporter*, p. 3.

"'Issues management' charts path as separate coordinating entity with formation of Issues Management Ass'n; Chase, Ewing elected leaders." (1982, April 12) *PR Reporter*, p. 1.

"Issues management: the corporation gets tough." (1982, June) *Management Review*, p. 4.

"'Issues management,' far from being a fad, continues to progress." (1982, May) *Impact*, p. 2.

"Issues mgmt. group founded. Rival to PRSA?" (1982, April 14) *Jack O'Dwyers Newsletter*, p. 3.

"Issues management: preparing for social change." (1981, October 28) *Chemical Week*, pp. 46-51.

Johnson, J. (1983, Fall) "Issues management: what are the issues?" *Business Quarterly*, pp. 22-31.

Jones, B. L., and W. H. Chase. (1979, Summer) "Managing public policy issues." *Public Relations Review*, pp. 3-23.

Kast, F. (1980, Fall) "Scanning the future environment: social indicators." *California Management Review*, pp. 22-32.

Katz, G. (1984, January 20) "He tracks news in and out." *USA Today*, p. 64.

Kefalas, A. G., and P. P. Schoderbek. (1973, No. 4) "Scanning the business environment — some empirical results." *Decision Sciences*, pp. 63-74.

Keim, G. D., C. P. Zeithaml, and B. D. Baysinger. (1984) "New directions for corporate political strategy." *Sloan Management Review*, pp. 53-62.

Kenner, J. (1987, Spring) "Can the IMA adapt and maintain its position of leadership?" *The 'IMA' Newsletter*, p. 7.

——. (1985, Summer) "Toward the USA corporation: the emerging linkages between public policy and company planning." *Futures Research Quarterly*, pp. 74-84.

Kiechel, W., III. (1982, December 27) "Corporate strategist under fire." *Fortune*, pp. 34-39.

Ladd, E. C. (1980, October 20) "How to tame the special-interest groups." *Fortune*, pp. 66-80.

Lauer, L. D. (1983, April) "Putting a lid on crises." *Case Currents,* pp. 38–39.

Lebart, F. T. (1982, November) "Campaigning on the issues." *Public Relations Journal,* pp. 30–33.

Lesly, P. (1981, December) "Functioning in the new human climate." *Management Review,* pp. 24–28.

Linneman, R. E., and H. E. Klein. (1985, January-February) "Using scenarios in strategic decision making." *Business Horizons,* pp. 64–74.

Little, C. H. (1986, Spring) "Who forecasts better—business people or professional forecasters?" *Futures Research Quarterly,* pp. 39–52.

Livingston, D. (1983, No. 2) "The issues of issues management." *New Jersey Bell Journal,* pp. 16–23.

Mahon, J. F. (1983, Autumn) "Corporate political strategy." *Business in the Contemporary World 2,* pp. 50–62.

Mahon, J. F., and S. A. Waddock. (1992) "Strategic issues management: an integration of issue life cycle perspectives." *Business and Society,* pp. 19–32.

Markley, O. W. (1983, February) "Preparing for the professional futures field." *Futures,* pp. 47–64.

Marx, T. G. (1990, February) "Strategic planning for public affairs." *Long Range Planning* (UK), pp. 9–16.

McCraw, T. K. (1975, Summer) "Regulation in America: a review article." *Business History Review,* pp. 159–183.

McMillan, C. J., and V. V. Murray. (1983, Summer) "Strategically managing public affairs: lessons from the analysis of business–government relations." *Business Quarterly,* pp. 94–100.

McNamee, M. (1983, May 23) "Scouting the future for danger." *USA Today,* p. 1.

Meng, M. (1992) "Early identification aids issues management." *Public Relations Journal,* pp. 22–24.

Menninger, E. J. (1984, March) "A case for strategic thinking." *Public Relations Journal,* p. 25.

Molitor, G. T. T. (1977, Summer) "How to anticipate public-policy changes." *Advanced Management Journal,* pp. 4–13.

"Monitoring and strategic planning move to proactive stance." (1983, April 18) *PR Reporter,* p. 3.

Moore, M. L. (1989, Summer) "Issue analysis, development, and management systems: parallel structures for public sector OD." *Public Administration Quarterly,* pp. 232–254.

Nagel, S. S. (1980, November-December) "Policy studies and futures research." *World Future Society Bulletin,* pp. 1–10.

Nelson, R. A. (1990, Spring) "Bias versus fairness: the social utility of issues management." *Public Relations Review,* pp. 25–32.

Neufeld, W. P. (1985, Fall) "Environmental scanning: its uses in forecasting emerging trends and issues in organizations." *Futures Research Quarterly,* pp. 39–52.

"The new breed of strategic planner." (1984, September 17) *Business Week,* pp. 62–68.

Nishi, K., C. Schoderbek, and P. P. Schoderbek. (1982, December) "Scanning the organizational environment: some empirical results." *Human Systems Performance,* pp. 233–245.

Nolan, J. T. (1985, May-June) "Political surfing when issues break." *Harvard Business Review,* pp. 72–81.

Oliver, A. R., and J. R. Garber. (1983, March-April) "Implementing strategic planning: 10 sure-fire ways to do it wrong." *Business Horizons,* pp. 49–51.

Pagan, R. D., Jr. (1986, Spring) "The Nestle boycott: implications for strategic business planning." *The Journal of Business Strategy,* pp. 12–18.

Parker, R. (1987, Spring) "Biggest problem for the issues manager doesn't pertain to issues." *The 'IMA' Newsletter,* p. 3.

Paul, K. (1981–82, Winter-Spring) "Business environment/public policy problems for the 1980s." *Business and Society,* pp. 11–16.

Perham, J. (1981, December) "New company watchdog." *Dun's Business Month,* pp. 88–89.

Perelman, L. J. (1983, Spring) "The value of business intelligence." *New Management,* pp. 30–35.

Pipho, C. (1987, Spring) "Examining the dilemma of issues management vis-a-vis education." *The 'IMA' Newsletter,* p. 8.

Post, J. E., E. A. Murray, Jr., R. B. Dickie, and J. F. Mahon. (1982, No. 2) "The public affairs function in American corporations: development and relations with corporate planning." *Long Range Planning,* pp. 12–21.

———. (1983, Fall) "Managing public affairs: the public affairs function." *California Management Review,* pp. 135–150.

Regan, P. J. (1981, November-December) "The importance of social and political trends." *Financial Analysts Journal,* pp. 10–11.

Reich, R. B. (1981, May-June) "Regulation by confrontation or negotiation?" *Harvard Business Review,* pp. 82–93.

Renfro, W. L. (1990, Fall) "Issues management: the American experience." *Journal of the International Public Relations Association,* pp. 17–19.

———. (1989, Fall) "How and why issues emerge: the changing role of the issues media." *Futures Research Quarterly,* pp. 71–81.

———. (1989, Fall) "How to build a foresight capability." *Association Management,* pp. 27–30.

———. (1989, August) "Anticipating and managing emerging public issues." *The Chinese Journal of Administration,* pp. 85–98.

———. (1987, November-December) "The lame duck legislature." *Vanguard,* pp. 5–6.

———. (1987, October) "Issues management: the evolving corporate role." *Futures,* pp. 545–554.

———. (1987, May-June) "Scenarios: a new approach." *Vanguard,* pp. 8–10.

———. (1987, Spring) "Cartoons communicate . . . with pun and punch!" *The 'IMA' Newsletter,* pp. 4–5.

———. (1987, March) "Future histories: a new scenario concept." *The Futurist,* pp. 28–33.

———. (1986, December) "Limits of governance: an emerging issue for the governors." In *The Future of State Government,* pp. 9–11. Lexington, Kentucky: Council of State Governments.

———. (1983, January) "Issues management." *GDI Impuls,* pp. 10–16.

———. (1982, August) "Managing the issues of the 1980s." *The Futurist,* pp. 61–66.

———. (1983, March) "The end of 'New Deal' values." *GDI Impuls,* pp. 29–36.

———. (1982, February) "Anticipating Congress." *Association Management,* pp. 163–165.

———. (1980, July) "Congress, corporations and crystal balls: a partnership for the future?" *Planning Review,* pp. 31–35.

——. (1980, August) "Forecasting the impact of public policies." *Long Range Planning,* pp. 80–89.

——. (1980, July-August) "Policy impact analysis: a step beyond forecasting." *Bulletin,* pp. 19–26.

——. (1978, April) "The future and congressional reform." *American Bar Association Journal,* pp. 561–563.

Renfro, W. L., and J. L. Morrison. (1984, August) "Detecting the signals of change." *The Futurist,* pp. 49–53.

——. (1982, October) "Merging two futures concepts: issues management and policy impact analysis." *The Futurist,* pp. 54–56.

Richardson, E. L. (1983) "Corporate planning in a changing Washington environment: divining and shaping the future." In *Effective Washington Representation,* ed. S. J. Marcuss, pp. 329–350. New York: New York Law and Business.

Roeser, T. F. (1981–82, Winter-Spring) "Identifying public affairs resources." *Business and Society,* pp. 7–10.

Schonfeld, E. P., and J. H. Boyd. (1982, February-March) "The financial payoff in corporate advertising." *Journal of Advertising Research,* pp. 45–55.

Sethi, S. P. (1977, Fall) "Advocacy advertising and the multinational corporation." *Columbia Journal of World Business,* pp. 33–46.

——. (1977, Spring) "Business and the news media: a paradox of informed misunderstanding." *California Management Review,* pp. 52–62.

——. (1979, January) "Institutional/image advertising and idea/issue advertising as policy tools: some public policy issues." *Journal of Marketing,* pp. 68–72.

——. (1976, Summer) "Management fiddles while public affairs flops." *Business and Society Review,* pp. 9–11.

Shanklin, W. L. (1979, October) "Strategic business planning: yesterday, today, and tomorrow." *Business Horizons,* pp. 7–14.

Simmons, W. W. (1979, November) "Issues management — challenge and opportunity for planning executives." *Planning Review,* pp. 15–19.

Steiner, J. F. (1977, April) "Business response to public distrust." *Business Horizons,* pp. 74–81.

"Strategic planning: determining the impact of environmental characteristics and uncertainty." (1982, September) *Academy of Management Journal,* pp. 500–509.

Stroup, M. A. (1986, February) "Issues management." *International Public Relations,* pp. 28–31.

Thain, D. H. (1980, Spring) "Improving competence to deal with politics and government: the management challenge of the '80s." *Business Quarterly,* pp. 31–45.

Thompson, D. B. (1981, February 23) "Issue management: new key to corporate survival." *Industry Week,* p. 77.

Tisdall, C. W. (1980, Autumn) "Communicating in the doubting '80s." *Business Quarterly,* pp. 82–87.

Vogel, D. (1979, April) "Ralph Naders all over the place." *Across the Board,* pp. 26–31.

"Volatility and vulnerability spur issues management." (1984, January) *Journal of the Scallop Companies,* pp. 1–3.

Wack, P. (1985, November-December) "Scenarios: shooting the rapids." *Harvard Business Review,* pp. 139–150.

Walker, J. L. (1983, No. 77) "The origins and maintenance of interest groups in America." *The American Political Science Review,* pp. 390–404.

Ward, B. (1983, January) "Thoughts for our tommorrows." *Delta Airlines Inflight Magazine,* pp. 44–46.

Wartick, S. L. (1986, Winter) "A tool for corporate public policy analysis." *Business Forum,* pp. 13–20.

Wayne, L. (1982, May 30) "Management gospel gone wrong." *New York Times.*

Weiner, E., and A. Brown. (1982, October) "Another wave of government regulation could be approaching." *Association Management,* pp. 161–163.

Werner, S. B. (1990) "The movement for reforming American business ethics: a twenty year perspective." *Journal of Business Ethics,* pp. 61–70.

"Why business got a bad name." (1976, Fall) *Business and Society Review,* pp. 10–27.

Williams, P. F. (1982) "Attitudes toward the corporation and the evaluation of social data." *Journal of Business Research,* pp. 119–131.

Williamson, O. E. (1981, December) "The modern corporation: origins, evolution, attributes." *Journal of Economic Literature,* pp. 1537–1568.

Wilson, L. J. (1990, Spring) "Corporate issues management: an international view." *Public Relations Review,* pp. 40–51.

Yoffie, D. B., and S. Bergenstein. (1985, Fall) "Creating political advantage: the rise of the corporate political entrepreneur." *California Management Review,* pp. 124–137.

Yovovich, B. G. (1983, May 23) "Tracking the trends in public opinion." *Advertising Age.*

Zenisek, T. J. (1979, July) "Corporate social responsibility: a conceptualization based on organizational literature." *Academy of Management Review,* pp. 359–368.

Zimmerman, J. (1983, March) "Learning to think in strategic terms." *International Management,* pp. 63–64.

PRIVATE REPORTS

Basche, J. (1981) *International Dimensions of Planning.* New York: The Conference Board.

Blank, S. (1980) *Assessing the Political Environment: An Emerging Function in International Companies.* New York: The Conference Board.

Brown, J. K. (1981) *Guidelines for Managing Corporate Issues Programs.* New York: The Conference Board.

——. (1979) *This Business of Issues: Coping with the Company's Environments.* New York: The Conference Board.

Coates, J. F., et al. (1986) *Issues Identification and Management: Developing a Research Agenda.* Palo Alto, Calif.: Electric Power Research Institute.

——. (1985, July) *Issues Identification and Management: The State of the Art Methods and Techniques.* Palo Alto, Calif.: Electric Power Research Institute.

——. (1986) *Issues Management: How You Can Plan, Organize, and Manage for the Future.* Mt. Airy, Md.: Lomond.

Ewing, R. P. (1981, April 27) *Allstate's Issues Management Committee, in Business, Economics and Social Trends.* Philadelphia: Human Resource Network.

——. (1981) *Chicago, the PCC and the Profession.* Chicago: The Publicity Club of Chicago.

———. (1983) *Issues Management: PR Comes of Age.* New York: Public Relations Society of America Counselors Academy.

Haendel, D. (1981) *Corporate Strategic Planning: The Political Dimension.* Washington, D.C.: Center for Strategic and International Studies, Georgetown University.

Hastings, A. H., J. Scanlon, and B. J. Hayward. (1985, August) *Strategies for Organizing Your Forecasting Function.* Washington, D.C.: Office of the Deputy Assistant Secretary for Health (Planning and Evaluation).

Heinz, L., and J. F. Coates. (1986) *Models for Issues Management: Superfund and RCRA as Test Cases.* Washington, D.C.: Edison Electric Institute.

Issues Management: The New Force in Business and Public Policy. (1985) Summary of proceedings of January 1985 conference. Oakland, Calif.: Clorox Company.

Lusterman, S. (1985) *Managing International Public Affairs.* New York: The Conference Board.

Michael, D. N., et al. (1980) *Values and Strategic Planning.* Menlo Park, Calif.: Stamford Research Institute International.

O'Connor, R. (1985) *Facing Strategic Issues: New Planning Guides and Practices.* New York: The Conference Board.

———. (1978) *Planning under Uncertainty: Multiple Scenarios and Contingency Planning.* New York: The Conference Board.

Ogilvy, J. A. (1984) *Social Issues and Trends: The Maturation of America.* Menlo Park, Calif.: Stamford Research Institute International.

Public Affairs Council. (1979) *The Fundamentals of Issues Management.* Washington, D.C.: The Council.

Renfro, W. L. (1983) *The Legislative Role of Corporations.* New York: AMACOM.

Snyder, D. P. (1979) *Demographic, Economic and Social Trends and Developments That Will Shape the Organizational Operating Environment during the 1980's.* Washington, D.C.: The Contemporary Speakers Bureau.

———. (1980) *Strategic Issues for the Eighties.* New York: Public Relations Society of America.

U.S. Congress, Foresight Task Force. (1983) *Foresight in the Private Sector: How Can Government Use It?* Washington, D.C.: U.S. Government Printing Office.

United Way of America, Strategic Planning Division. (1984) *Scenarios, a Tool for Planning in Uncertain Times.* Alexandria, Va.: United Way.

UNPUBLISHED PAPERS

Keegan, W. J. (1967) "Scanning the international business environment: a study of the information acquisition process." Ph.D. diss., Harvard University.

Kefalas, A. G. (1971) "Scanning the external business environment." Ph.D. diss., University of Iowa.

McConnell, D. (1983) "Emerging situations surveillance and corporate issues management." Working paper, University of Maine.

PUBLISHED SPEECHES

Anderson, W. C. (1983, November 7) "The conflicting interests within a multidivisional organization in developing an issue response." Presented before the

Issues Management Association.

Armstrong, P. A. (1981, October) "The concept and practice of issues management in the United States." *Vital Speeches,* pp. 763–765.

Chase, W. H. (1984, October 16) "Issue management: origins of the future." Presented before the Public Affairs Section of the Public Relations Society of America, Denver.

Connor, F. J. (1983, November 7) "Issues management at American Can Company." Presented before the Issues Management Association.

Edgar, R. (1984, May 30) "The future of public-private cooperation." Presented before the Issues Management Association.

Ewing, R. P. (1983, November 7) "The future of issues management and the role of IMA." Presented before the Issues Management Association.

Geist, J. D. (1983, November 8) "The new components of change." Presented before the Issues Management Association.

Gotlieb, A. E. (1984, May 31) "Canada-U.S. relations: problem solving and dispute settlement." Presented before the Issues Management Association.

Haayen, R. J. (1982, May 13) "The corporation and the urban dilemma: an insider's view." Presented before the National College of Education, Evanston, Ill.

Hagstrom, J. (1984, May) "The shifting balance." Presented before the Issues Management Association, Washington, D.C.

Lukaszewski, James E. (1992, February 1) "Managing fear." *Vital Speeches,* p. 238.

———. (1991, June 15) "It ain't easy being green." *Vital Speeches,* p. 532.

———. (1990, July 1) "Managing bad news in America." *Vital Speeches,* p. 568.

Michael, D. L. (1986, Summer) "Reaching senior management: a series of observations." *Futures Research Quarterly,* pp. 81–86.

Pace, N. (1982, November 18) "A board member examines issues management." Presented before the Issues Management Association.

Pagan, R. D. (1986, February) "Business ethics and the churches." *International Public Relations,* pp. 17–19.

———. (1983, November 7) "Issue management: no set path." Presented before the Issues Management Association.

———. (1983, October 25) "Issues management: the shaping of an issues strategy." Presented before the Public Relations Student Society of America, New York City.

Pollock, J. C. (1984, April 3) "The quiet revolution: what ordinary Americans are doing about fear of crime." Presented before the Second Annual Governor's Conference on Crime Protection, Albany, N.Y.

Renfro, William L. (1992, May 1) "Ratify the Second Amendment." *Vital Speeches,* pp. 429–431.

———. (1989, November 15) "The 100th Congress: a lame duck." *Vital Speeches,* pp. 95–97.

———. (1987, July 15) "Business government relations: a new paradigm." Speech to the Public Issues Forum of the Brookings Institution.

Index

ABOUT THE AUTHOR

WILLIAM L. RENFRO is President of the Policy Analysis Co., Inc. A founder of the Issues Management Association, he is a Director and its President. He is an international author and lecturer with articles in such journals as *The American Bar Association Journal, The Atlantic Monthly, International Public Relations Review* (London), *Futuribles* (Paris), *The Futurist,* and *The Chinese Journal of Administration* (Republic of China). He is the author or coauthor of six books, and has authored more than 60 guest Op-Ed columns on emerging issues for newspapers throughout the world.

DATE DUE

AUG 3 1 1994	
MAR 0 2 1995	
APR 2 2 1995	
82895	
DEC 1 1 199	
APR 0 3 1997	
APR 2 2 1997	
MAY 2 0 1998	
FEB 1 7 2003	

GAYLORD   PRINTED IN U.S.A.